4.95

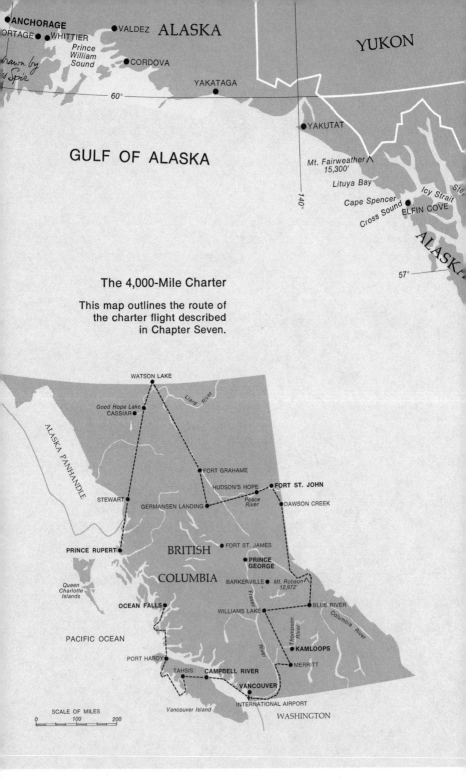

ANCHORAGE
PORTAGE • WHITTIER
VALDEZ
ALASKA

YUKON

Prince
William
Sound

CORDOVA

drawn by
s Spir

YAKATAGA

60°

YAKUTAT

GULF OF ALASKA

Mt. Fairweather ∧
15,300'

Lituya Bay

140°

Cape Spencer
Cross Sound
Icy Strait
ELFIN COVE

Ste

ALASK

57°

The 4,000-Mile Charter

This map outlines the route of
the charter flight described
in Chapter Seven.

WATSON LAKE

Liard River

Good Hope Lake
CASSIAR

ALASKA PANHANDLE

FORT GRAHAME

HUDSON'S HOPE
FORT ST. JOHN

STEWART
GERMANSEN LANDING
Peace
River
DAWSON CREEK

PRINCE RUPERT

FORT ST. JAMES

BRITISH

PRINCE
GEORGE

COLUMBIA

BARKERVILLE
Mt. Robson ∧
12,972'

Queen
Charlotte
Islands

OCEAN FALLS
WILLIAMS LAKE
BLUE RIVER
Columbia River

Fraser

Thompson River

River

PACIFIC OCEAN

PORT HARDY
KAMLOOPS

MERRITT

TAHSIS
CAMPBELL RIVER

VANCOUVER

SCALE OF MILES
0   100   200

Vancouver Island
INTERNATIONAL AIRPORT
WASHINGTON

British Columbia's Pacific Coast . . .

You will assist your understanding of the contents by using this specially-prepared map as reference. It contains only those places mentioned in the text.

MAGNETIC NORTH

BRITISH

COLUMBIA

ALBEK

PACIFIC OCEAN

Queen Charlotte Islands

Vancouver Island

WASHING

WRANGELL
STEWART
HYDER
NDLE
KETCHIKAN
Portland Canal
Union Lake
Union Inlet
TERRACE
Kitimat Arm
KITIMAT
PRINCE RUPERT
Triple Island
Rose Spit
Digby Island
McCauly Island
Douglas Channel
Porcher Island
Petrel Channel
MASSET
Ogden Channel
Grenville Channel
Principe Channel
USKATLA
Barnard Harbour
BUTEDALE
Graham Reach
Graham Island
Gill Island
Princess Royal Island
OTTE CITY
Compania Island
Laredo Inlet
te Channel
SANDSPIT
Otter Channel
Pooley Island
Trutch Island
Mathieson Channel
KLEMTU
Don Peninsula
Ethelda Bay
BELLA COOLA
TASU
Laredo Channel
Bentinck Arm
Chilko Lake
Dorothy Lake
Swindle Island
OCEAN FALLS
Cousins Inlet
Moresby Island
Florence Peninsula
Franklyn Arm
Good Hope Mtn. 10,362'
JEDWAY
BELLA BELLA
Gunboat Passage
Moses Inlet
Mt. Waddington 13,260'
Kunghit Island
Fisher Channel
NAMU
Rivers Inlet
Mt. Grenville 10,200'
Cape St. James
52°
Calvert Island
Boswell Inlet
Southgate River
Fitz Hugh Sound
Seymour Inlet
Bute Inlet
Menzies Bay
130°
Cape Caution
SULLIVAN BAY
MINSTREL ISLAND
STEWART ISLAND
Seymour Narrows
Toba Inlet
MANSONS LANDING
PORT HARDY
Johnstone Strait
ROBERTS C
COAL HARBOUR
ALERT BAY
Savary Island
GIBSON
Rupert Arm
Cortes Island
POWELL RIVER
LANDIN
Quatsino Sound
PORT ALICE
ZEBALLOS
Bowen Isl
Cape Cook
TAHSIS
CAMPBELL RIVER
VANCOL
Checleset Bay
KYUOQUOT
PENDER HARBOUR
ESPERANZA
GOLD RIVER
SECHELT
Nootka Island
FRIENDLY COVE
ALBERNI
INTERNATIO AIRPORT
Muchalat Arm
TOFINO
49°
VICTORIA
Juan de Fuca
Cape Flattery

SCALE OF MILES
0   50   100   150   200

The

Pathless

Way

"But follow me:
 Let me before you lay
 Rules for the flight,
 And mark the pathless way."

Ovid, 8 A.D.

THE

PATHLESS

WAY

by Justin de Goutiere

J. J. DOUGLAS LTD., VANCOUVER

First published in hardback by Graydonald Graphics Ltd., West Vancouver in 1968 and reprinted in 1969.
This edition first published by J.J. Douglas Ltd. in 1972.
Second paperback printing.

J.J. Douglas Ltd.
1875 Welch Street
North Vancouver, B.C. V7P 1B7

Canadian Shared Cataloguing in Publication Data

Goutiere, Justin de, 1926-1968.
    The pathless way

    ISBN 0-88894-006-8 pa.

        1. Goutiere, Justin de, 1926-1968.
2. Air pilots — British Columbia — Biography.
I. Title.
TL540.G69A3   629.13'092

Printed and bound in Canada by the Hunter Rose Company
Cover art direction by Mike Yazzolino
Cover art by Carl Chaplin

  Page

CHAPTER ONE
    Flying the Frontier - - - - - - - -   1

CHAPTER TWO
    The Good Friday Disaster - - - - - -   14

CHAPTER THREE
    "Thar She Blows!" - - - - - - - -   33

CHAPTER FOUR
    Stuck in the Mud - - - - - - - -   44

CHAPTER FIVE
    I Take a Short Cut - - - - - - - -   53

CHAPTER SIX
    Zero Zero Seven Versus Zero Seven Zero -   62

CHAPTER SEVEN
    Charters Are Fun . . . Sometimes - - - -   78

CHAPTER EIGHT
    Airborne Ambulance - - - - - - -   116

CHAPTER NINE
    Crossing Hecate Strait - - - - - - -   124

CHAPTER TEN
    Hangar Talk - - - - - - - - - -   140

CHAPTER ELEVEN
    Accidents Happen - - - - - - - -   161

CHAPTER TWELVE
    Closing the Hangar Doors - - - - - -   177

FOREWORD

I WAS A COMMERCIAL AIRCRAFT PILOT who flew light aircraft almost 20 years. I was asked a lot of questions. Principally, there were two: why did I fly and why did I like flying a light aircraft on the rough coast of British Columbia?

Now retired, for the first time there has been a chance for some soul-searching: why *did* I fly and why *did* I like the B.C. coast so much?

The answers lie in these chapters. They are phrased in airman's language because it is the only one I know now.

During my analysis I came to the conclusion there was another answer beyond what you will read here. On the ground, I was a typical husband and father who washed the car on Sundays (when schedules permitted), cut the grass, fretted over five growing boys, mixed a good martini and thought he was hell on a barbecue. I also love my wife. At the same time, I was having a hot affair with an airplane so long now it seems forever. She filled me with a strange passion the instant I was airborne. It was the knowing of every friendly instrument, the familiar scratch on the inside of the windscreen, the sound of two engines in harmony, the perfume of oil, fuel and leather, the musical plink of ripples on the floats, the sense of well-being. Airborne, it was a love affair supplanting everything else.

A good commercial pilot is no good, not commercial, nor a pilot if he is ever unfaithful to his aerial mistress. When that happens he should turn in his ticket because trouble is ahead.

This requires a wife who understands for if she does not there will be dissension at home, as many airmen know well. My Anna has understood and I dedicate this book to her in gratitude.

Not many pilots can write and there are fewer writers who can fly. Combining the two abilities has been a task for me. Rather than explaining the questions with a long editorial, I have chosen the pathless way of anecdote and illustration. It is but an average cross-section of only one coast pilot's career.

This book does not extoll the beauty of the British Columbia coast. It has been described many times by writers more professional and any attempt of mine would be amateur. Of course the coast is beautiful—raw, primitive, untrammelled beauty that once experienced lingers forever in memory like incense. It is a true handiwork of God. From above on a clear day when the sky is blue, punctuated by fleecy clouds, it is soul-stirring. But those days when flying is easy do not make anecdotes. The challenges come when the fog banks roll, the rain beats and the wind takes charge. Seek elsewhere if you want to read about the coastal beauty. I have tried to depict the awesome side of its split personality that you may understand the fascination of challenging it with small aircraft.

I hope you like my second love.

J. de G.

Flying
the Frontier

BRITISH COLUMBIA is geography's complete expression and the Pacific shoreline is its supreme gift. From San Diego, California, to Cape Flattery on Washington's Olympic Peninsula, there are only six harbours of any size and security in 1300 miles of coast—Long Beach, Monterey, San Francisco Bay, Eureka, Willapa Bay and Gray's Harbour. All the rest is pounding surf.

What a geological wonder it is, to cross the international boundary in the Strait of Juan de Fuca into another country, another world—almost another time. From Juan de Fuca to the Portland Canal north of Prince Rupert, where the Alaska Panhandle boundary begins there are 17,000 miles of indented coastline in the 525 mile length. Every average mile holds 33 miles of shore.

How can words convey the magnificence of the panorama—sheen or shadow? tranquillity or tempest?

symmetry or schism? inviting or forbidding? Stephen Leacock said: "If I had known what it was like, I wouldn't have been content with a mere visit. I'd have been born there." A British Chancellor of the Exchequer wrote in 1842: "Bounded by frost and banked by fog, woe betide any unfortunate individual who might be so far diverted from the path of prudence to settle in these parts." And a contemporary poet calls it, "a slow smash in the eye."

The B.C. coast is what you make it. It is benign to the retired, challenging to the young, satisfying to the creative. As Rudyard Kipling said: "Such a land is good for an energetic man. It is also not so bad for the loafer."

A fledgling author can search months seeking descriptions by other men and never discover the satisfactorily complete answer. Nature has bestowed the coast with such generosity she has beggared man's ability to explain it adequately.

Hidden within a Queen's Printer-published bulletin, *Landforms of British Columbia*, I discovered this sensitive paragraph: "The fiords of the mainland rank in size and scenic grandeur with the world-famous fiord coastlines of Norway, Patagonia and the South Island of New Zealand. The fiords are half a mile to two miles wide and have steep glaciated sides that rise from the water's edge in long unbroken slopes to summits at 6,000 to 8,000 feet. Along their length, water cascades over falls and down rock faces, and landslides on steep slopes frequently have bared the granitic rocks of all vegetation. On clear days when the all too prevalent low clouds are swept away, the scenery among the many lonely fiords is majestic." Thank you, Dr. Stuart Holland, government geologist-author.

You can take a cruise up the coast, poke about the inlets, walk as far from the ship as the end of the dock, look up at the enveloping mountains, shrug your mist-sodden shoulders and say to hell with it, who needs it, and flee. As one unknown has been quoted: "You've got the scenery, you've got the timber—but I'm going back east where the money is." Or you can say to yourself, by God this is a man's country, accept the challenge and stay.

More have stayed than are leaving and small aircraft have made possible their communication. The quiet reaches delving deep into the mountain fastness are still remote and lonely but the light plane and the shortwave radio have killed the isolation forever. No part of the coast is now more than two hours flight time from urban life and services. Almost every settlement is linked to the world by radio-telephone. Vancouver newspapers are read along its length next day.

Once there was a doughty fleet of ships crewed by rugged men who first brought the start of life and then kept the outports alive with a weekly cargo of necessities. In recent years the marine service has abdicated almost completely in favor of aircraft and their dedicated companies which have accepted the responsibility for the life of the coast.

Before you can understand the following, I think it pertinent, if the class will pay attention, to take a short course on the coast. As they say: "Ya gotta know the territory."

Once upon a time, about 108 million years ago, there was a land mass west of the present coastline and the present mainland was under the sea. Geologists call it Cascadia. Then, 25 million years ago, the Rockies and the mainland having been formed 40 million years

3

earlier, Cascadia sank to leave above the surface only Vancouver Island, the Queen Charlotte Islands and the smaller offshore islands. This was nature's first of many gifts to British Columbia. Without the breakwaters of those islands, the mainland coast behind them would not possess its present fiord-havens. It was a two-fold gift—not only topographic, but climatic. As the water-laden Pacific winds sweep easterly, the island mount-ain ridges are the first high ground they meet in 6,000 miles. Up goes the air, down comes the rain and up go the big trees. There is enough left for the seaward side of the Coast mountains to get a yearly drenching before the unburdened winds pass to the prairies.

There was a negative side to the gift. It created an area unlike any other on the continent behind a barrier that has kept it too long removed from the stream of progress. Even the Indians were different. Like birds and animals which adapt to their regions, the coast Indians became fishermen. They moved by sea, they lived from it and their gods were of it. They became lost inland. While other Indian inland nations became hunters and bushmen, the coast Indians became watermen in their 80-ft. cedar dugouts, navigating out of sight of land as the Haida did when they swept down from the Charlottes to make war on Vancouver Island. They were more Polynesian than North American. I have always thought the name "Indian" too general.

Then in 1778, two little ships, *Resolution* and *Discovery* came over the Pacific horizon from the Sand-wich Islands, bearing Captain James Cook and crew who became the first white men to land on the coast. This happened at Nootka on the west coast of Van-couver Island. The coming was long overdue. It was the enlightened reign of George III, the time of Samuel

Johnson and Sir Walter Scott, Goldsmith, Shelley, Burns, Keats, Gainsborough, Reynolds and Wedgewood: the introduction of steam, the first industrial machinery like the spinning frame and the spinning jenny. It was two years after the Declaration of American Independence. New York's first newspaper had been printed 53 years before. Montreal's Chateau de Ramezay was already a 73-year old building. Yet on the coast the years of discovery were just beginning. Today, it might be compared to a National Geographic Society expedition finding still-unexplored territory in New Guinea.

One of Cook's midshipmen was a 20-year old boy, George Vancouver. In 1791, by now a commander, he was charged by the British Admiralty with a double mission—take over the territory at Nootka Sound, handed to England by the Nootka Convention of 1790, and survey the North Pacific coast. For three years, 1792 to 1794, he explored and surveyed and went around Vancouver Island. His original charts exist today and are remarkably accurate. Many of the channels, inlets and islands are named after the men of his crew. So the coast remained for another half century, principally on paper, in the far away chart room of the British Admiralty.

During the time George Vancouver was on the coast, the North West Company's Alexander MacKenzie reached saltwater on Bentinck Arm, in 1793, overland from the east. He became the first explorer to cross the continent north of Mexico. Fur trade developers followed from the east, but only a few expeditions like Simon Fraser's, reached the coast. Most of the fur traffic out of the interior country went east across the prairie to the Great Lakes and Montreal, or down the

Columbia river to the Pacific.

In 1820, a 17-year old Scot, James Douglas, arrived in the interior fur trade country and in 1840 the Hudson's Bay company made him chief factor of all territory west of the Rockies. Three years later, he built Fort Victoria on Vancouver Island. Thus, in 1843, contemporary life began on the coast. It was Douglas, governor of Vancouver Island in 1851, governor of the mainland colony in 1858 and governor of British Columbia until 1864, knighted for services to the Queen in 1863, who brought law, a semblance of order and the first glimmer of civilization to the new territory and the old coast.

It was just a glimmer. In 1858, gold was found in the Fraser River sandbars. That summer, a flood of 20,000 men arrived from California, China and the east, heading for the interior where Billy Barker took $600,000 in nuggets from Wells Creek. The find resulted in an interior city that became the largest north of San Francisco, west of Chicago. The coast had to wait awhile longer.

It was a wait of another 35 years until 1897, when another gold rush this time to the Klondike, took 18,000 men up the B.C. coast in barques, steam boats and in hulls almost derelict. Many a would-be Klondiker lost his life by shipwreck on the rocks, mostly because the skippers had no knowledge of the tidal waters. It was the Klondike that was responsible for the coast's first settlers and its first settlements, little more than a half century ago.

Gradually, there came fish canneries surrounded by fishermen's houses, logging camps on shore and afloat with nearby sawmills, a paper mill at Ocean Falls, another at Powell River. The Gibson brothers began a lumber mill at Tahsis on the west coast of Vancouver Island and around in the next inlet gold was discovered at Zeballos. Little by little, life grew on the coast, nurtured by tough men. There were still hundreds of miles of lonesome, uninhabited shoreline between the settlements, and to supply them in the pre-World War II years, small steamships most all out of Vancouver, itself growing fast, shuttled among the outports on schedule, keeping the coast alive, etching their names forever in the memories of the people.

The C.P.R. fleet poked its yellow and black funnels into every inlet. Union Steamship's red and black stacks traded them off. It was a 'you take one, I'll take the next one' arrangement. Many places had no docks and passengers and freight were lightered ashore. For such ports of call there were special doors off the cargo decks just above the water. In fog, the ships navigated by dead reckoning and whistle-blowing, timing the echo's return. On flat reefs too low to ricochet an echo, stood hoardings that looked like billboards without advertising, to bounce the whistle sound. The coast's remoteness was retreating. At the same time, activity was restricted to around the ports of call.

Then began the first timorous flights by a few daring aviators who went into the unknown without benefit of weather information. Their radios wouldn't work over a 100 miles and then only in the best of conditions.

Steamer travel remained the principal method through the World War II years and for a period afterward. Vancouverites going to Victoria, reserved berths on the C.P.R.'s nightly "night boat" which left Pier D in Vancouver at midnight and travelled half speed to arrive in Victoria at seven next morning. For many it was the first night of a honeymoon. The night boats were always packed to the life boats and those who couldn't get berths had to make out on the leather chairs in the lounges. Offices worked until Saturday noon and at 2 o'clock, 14 Union Steamship Co. vessels, *Lady Alexandra, Lady Evelyn, Lady Cynthia* and the others, would trail out First Narrows, line astern, each bound for a different port upcoast, packed with weekenders headed for their summer camps. They were all back in Vancouver by Sunday midnight.

To train crews, the Air Force built a seaplane base at Jericho in Vancouver's English Bay. A patrol base was built at Tofino on the west coast of Vancouver Island, another at Coal Harbour on the Island, and another at Seal Cove, Prince Rupert. There were airstrips at Port Hardy on the east side of the Island and at Sandspit on the Queen Charlottes. That was it. Anyone who flew the coast on business when a steamship was available, caught hell from his wife for in every sense it was strictly "seat of the pants" flying.

The aviation breakthrough came in '48-'49 when the Aluminum Company of Canada began construction of Kitimat that was to become known around the world as the "instant town". It created so much traffic out of Vancouver, any machine with wings and a propellor, and a pilot crazy enough, floundered its way to the giant site. Canadian Pacific Airlines started scheduled flights to Kitimat using DC3's out of Vancouver. Of necessity, there were two stops on the way, at Port Hardy and Sandspit. There the passengers transferred to a Canso amphibian flying boat, were flown across Hecate Strait to Prince Rupert to make their way from there to Kitimat by road or rail. As well, there was a semi-scheduled operation to the construction by Queen Charlotte Airlines and Pacific Western Airlines using wartime Canso's and pre-war Straney double-winged flying boats. The two merged later to become Pacific Western and that Vancouver-based company is now Canada's third largest airline after Air Canada and CP Air.

Majority of the flights were chartered and a motley conglomeration of aircraft was used—two-place J3 Cub's, Aeronca's, side by side Luscombe's, Sea Bee's, Norsemen, old Fairchild's, Stinson's, Fleet Canucks and new at that time, Cessna 104's—none of them except the Norseman, designed for the work they were doing. It was the perfect time to introduce the de Haviland Beaver. For bush work it has never been bettered. None of them, relatively speaking, carried radios, because there wasn't anybody to communicate with. Radio wasn't necessary, even at the Vancouver airport. A pilot just waggled his wings on the way in and watched for a green light signal from the tower.

Vancouver to Kitimat is about 525 miles and the distance required establishing three fuel stops on the route. Manson's Landing, Minstrel Island and Sullivan Bay became the stop off points for hundreds and hundreds of passengers and pilots who flew the coast adventurously just 20 years ago. Manson's Landing, sited on the southwest side of Cortes Island at the northwestern end of the Strait of Georgia, is a sheltered little harbour and in the summer months it is an active boaters' marina. The little rustic coffee shop and the cabins in the pines along the shore bear no resemblance today to the earlier activity. On the wall of the shop is a well-worn Cessna Crane wooden propellor. On it are hundreds of signatures of the pilots of those days. Some are now "million milers", captains of jet airliners for major companies around the world. Some have retired, some are still flying the coast and some have become accident statistics in Department of Transport records.

The story of B.C. Air Lines Ltd. best illustrates the growth of coastal aerial communication. By coincidence it is the company for which I piloted six and a half years until my retirement from active flying. Throughout this book you will read many references to "the company" and this is the one to which I refer. Its beginning was no different than many others. Incorporated in '43, it was inactive until '46 because of the lack of equipment and pilots in wartime. That year it acquired two Luscombe's on floats, and for a long period afterward the little operation begged for gas money. By 1952, there was a Waco, two Beaver's, four Luscombe's, a Piper Super-Cruiser, a Piper Clipper, a Stinson 108, a Globe Swift, a Fairchild 71 and six Sea Bee's, eighteen in all—and in Vancouver the company was running a flying school. The passenger capacity was 51.

Ten years later in '62, there were 27 aircraft—three Grumman Mallard's, one Grumman Goose, five amphibian Beaver's, six float Beaver's, seven Cessna 180's and two of the original 170's. The passenger capacity was 157. The pilots were wearing uniforms instead of baseball caps and baggy slacks. There were 10 major bases from Vancouver to Prince Rupert and the company had become known as the world's unique air service because 1) it was entirely sea plane or amphibian, 2) while it served 400 points of call all on the coast, and carried around 100,000 passengers a year, the average time of any flight was only 20 minutes duration. The other aspect that made the company unique was that all flights were under Visual Flight Regulations, in sight of water or land. Since the B.C.

coast is not notorious for its hours of sunshine or clear weather it makes for cruddy going most of the time.

You might ask the question: "Why not fly on instruments?" Flying to Instrument Flight Regulations demands land-based radio navigational aids and since it was only a few years ago when ships navigated in fog by hooting at cliffsides, radio beacons on the coast are still few and far between. But to serve the points of call we do, ("veer right at the end of the inlet and land by the second log boom on the left") the ability to fly on instruments is secondary to a sure knowledge of every finger of water, rock, tree and landmark on the whole 17,000 mile shoreline. On this coast it is necessary for survival that a pilot is able any time, in any weather, in any circumstance, to know his precise location.

Every day is different—air ambulance service for the seriously ill or injured, charters to places off the usual routes, freight, mail, break-down parts for heavy mining, logging or fishing equipment—it is a mixed bag. There are the regular schedules out of Vancouver to Ocean Falls and points on Vancouver Island, and out of Prince Rupert to the Queen Charlotte Islands and south as far as Ocean Falls. Then there are the shuttle services, transporting passengers from the outports to a main base where they can board a CP Air or PWA airliner flight. A unique example of a scheduled flight is the one from Prince Rupert to Port Hardy and return. That flight requires 18 take-offs and landings, carrying passengers and freight, most of the time in weather when smart ducks stay grounded. Tricky and fickle, the coast weather can be grand one minute, zero zero the next. Eighty mile an hour winds are not uncommon but the company's safety record is second to none.

In 1965, the company began training IFR pilots

so scheduled flights into Vancouver could be performed under IFR conditions. It happens often that a flight will be delayed because conditions at that end are socked in. With IFR pilots, flights need be cancelled no longer. In 1967, wheels-only aircraft were added to the fleet, to be used out of Vancouver to the air fields at Tofino, Bella Coola, Mica Creek, Kamloops and for charter. Now the company has 200 radio stations on the coast plus 150 others, privately owned. The rain-swept dock-floats have been replaced by nice waiting rooms with ready coffee. In 1959, we were chosen to fly the Queen and Prince Philip during part of their Canadian tour.

This is not a book subsidized by the company, but to illustrate the point further, here is the company's record for 1967: its aircraft flew 6,472,360 revenue miles; carried 90,677 ton miles of freight and mail; transported 92,317 passengers; made 200 emergency mercy flights; served 400 coastal points; employed 140 people of whom 40 are pilots and 52 are maintenance personnel.

The point is—it is only 22 years. This is but one example of the way the coast is changing, of the way it is becoming part of the mainstream at last, of the major role light aircraft are playing in providing most of the coastal communication that is so vital to its growth.

It is only 176 years since Capt. Vancouver first charted the coast, 72 years since the Klondikers called attention to it, 22 years since aircraft started beating back the wilderness to make it possible for people to live and work in it without sacrificing contact with the world outside.

Now there is no coastal fleet of Canadian Pacific Steamships, the Union boats have been scrapped and only Northland Navigation Ltd. and the Alaska Cruise ships, make scheduled runs up the Inside Passage by-passing all the little places which used to depend on the marine highway. Aircraft have taken over almost completely.

This is the scene and the background to this book. Now that you know the territory, class is dismissed.

The Good Friday Disaster

FRIDAY, MARCH 27, 1964, WAS GOOD FRIDAY and the first reports originated by an Anchorage, Alaska, ham operator were sketchy. Confirmation came at midnight. By 3 a.m. it was established that a large area of coastal Alaska in the vicinity of Anchorage and a number of surrounding communities had experienced a major disaster with great damage and loss of life.

In the next immediate days the world was to learn that Alaska had been rocked by the strongest earthquake ever recorded in North America, but with a surprisingly low death toll of only 66. When compared to the earthquake in Iran that took 11,000 lives in 1968, San Francisco's of 1906 that killed 452 and the one in China in 1556 that accounted for 830,000 lives, Alaska's toll was light.

The Good Friday earthquake lifted more than 25,000 square miles of Alaska from three to eight inches. An island near Anchorage rose thirty-three feet and exposed a strip of sea floor 1350 feet wide. At the same time, a 3500 square mile area around Anchorage and Kodiak sank two to six feet. In Anchorage itself some parts fell 30 feet in a few seconds.

The shock waves rolled round the world. In Iran the surface rose and fell a third of an inch. Streets in Houston, Texas, rose five inches. Well water in Georgia moved up and down well shafts ten to twenty feet. In Mississippi, a showboat was torn from its mooring. In Alaska, more than 9200 after-shock quakes were recorded in the following six months. Along the Pacific coast, tidal waves flashed up the funnel of the Alberni Canal and smashed into the twin towns of Alberni and Port Alberni causing extensive destruction. They did it again at Crescent City on the California coast and washed some onlookers off the beach to drown.

At Prince Rupert where I was stationed, all under-sea cable connections between the city and the airport on Digby Island were cut. Big log booms stored in and around the harbour were broken, requiring weeks of salvage operations to gather. Many fish boats were pulled from their moorings and damaged.

Early next morning there was an emergency city council meeting and from it came the offer to provide whatever medical supplies, doctors and nurses Anchorage might need. Via a hastily supplemented radio network, Alaska Civil Defence officials declined because, they said, their U.S. Army units had the situation in control. I had indicated to council my aircraft was at its disposal if required but it now seemed the offer would not be needed.

At 10 a.m., my downtown agent had a phone call from Andy Marquis. As news director of the CTV

Vancouver television station, CHAN-TV, he was urgently requesting immediate charter of an aircraft to the earthquake area. I made a fast call to the base to have the ship serviced and ready to depart Rupert for Anchorage within the hour. Using Alaska Coastal-Ellis Airlines teletype, I made arrangements for clearing Customs at Juneau and I gathered the air charts of the area and advised my Vancouver head office.

We were airborne at 11:05. Marquis had Garvin McMinn with him, his newsreel photographer. Canadian Pacific Airlines had brought them up from Vancouver the night before and because of the Good Friday holiday they were without cash. Five minutes after takeoff, Marquis leaned across and said between them they had twelve bucks. He asked if it would cover the cost of the charter. I told him it would pay for maybe one dinner in Anchorage. I was a little short too—about $75—and I had to swipe my wife's housekeeping money to make up part.

The Alaska Panhandle weather information was thorough and had been supplied me by Coastal-Ellis. I had some difficulty between Prince Rupert and Ketchikan, a 90-mile leg, because of rain and sleet squalls with occasional fog banks. There was no wind. Marquis had begun to look anxious. Soon he was to realize how mild it was in comparison to what lay ahead. I was flying two to three hundred feet above the water and the visibility was bad. McMinn was disappointed at not being able to shoot some scenics as we proceeded up the spectacular coastline.

Past Ketchikan, the weather continued poor as it did past Wrangell and the historic town of Petersburg, 200 miles north of Prince Rupert. Going up Fredericks Sound and Stephens Passage, the weather worsened and we encountered moderate snow all the way to Juneau. The numerous non-directional radio beacons located up and down the Panhandle were invaluable in getting through to Juneau. While I had flown the route many times, this was the first in adverse weather and the job was made tougher since radio communications with the Prince Rupert base didn't exist, due to the low altitude.

After circling Juneau, the water landing was routine and U.S. Customs cleared us quickly. Juneau is 285 miles northwest of Prince Rupert point to point, but in following the channels my actual distance was 360 miles. By Prince Rupert time we arrived at 13:35. For the purpose of the log book records I stayed on Pacific Standard time for the whole trip but it was to cause confusion later.

I had a talk with the Coastal-Ellis pilots and dispatchers while the ship was being refuelled, and learned the weather between Juneau and Cape Spencer was poor and due to fog, several of their aircraft had been unable to reach Elfin Cove 30 miles up. There was no weather information available for the coast from the Cape on to Anchorage because of the communication breakdown between the different airfields en route. They were most helpful and gave me their maps. My passengers were anxious to press on so despite the gloomy weather outlook I decided to attempt as far as Cape Spencer.

Departing Juneau at 14:20 in moderate to heavy snow, I immediately ran into severe difficulties in the Gustavus region of the Icy Straits. Once, we circled a small island three times at wavetop level before heading out to Cross Sound. There was near zero visibility and for three or four minutes I had to keep that tiny rock pinnacle in sight as my only check point. Using the ADF, which was tuned to the Cape Spencer beacon, I was able to skirt between snow showers. Suddenly we rounded the Cape right on course for Yakutat, my next proposed fuel stop 200 miles further up.

The weather was still far from good but I picked up a lovely tail wind that I calculated was providing a 180 mile an hour ground speed. Then began the long but interesting trip up the rugged coastline. We flew the distance at altitudes between 300 and 800 feet in visibility at times near zero and at others in sun. The scenery was breathtaking. There were long stretches of black sand beaches broken by the tall rock outcroppings where the Pacific breakers piled with tremendous force to send the spray hundreds of feet into the air to be caught by the wind and driven inland in lacy drifts.

About 30 miles above the Cape a peculiar glow loomed on the shoreline. Marquis was fascinated. McMinn knelt on the sill between the seats and between us there was awed silence as we closed. It was the Mount Fairweather glacier and its glow was shedding an eerie light. We slipped along its face at 300 feet altitude just above where the ice met ocean. It must have been 100 feet thick and exposed boulders and sand dirtied the face. Great crevices threaded back from the face as far as we could see. The sun appeared just then and the crevice edges turned turquoise. Looking up the glacier where it vanished in the clouds, it became a treasure of turquoise diamonds sparkling on the ice. Directly ahead, a great slab fell from the face, broke into millions of pieces and vanished into the surf. McMinn was swearing because his camera was loaded with black and white film.

The glacier base, about four miles long, quickly

passed from view and so did everything else for once again we were flying through the murky tomb of a snow squall. After passing Lituya Bay we broke out into sun, allowing me to straighten the course and not have to follow every blessed cove, bay and headland as I had been forced to do. Occasionally, there were groups of moose or caribou close to the water. My passengers slept the rest of the way to Yakutat and only wakened when I was circling the field two miles inland from the ocean. It was a routine landing with the snow piled ten feet high along the runway.

Instructing the attendant to fuel up, I hurried into the weather office hoping to get some en route weather information. To my chagrin I was told the next airport, 80 miles northwest of Yakataga, had been badly damaged and the runway was unserviceable. There was no weather dope on Anchorage. The suggestion was made to proceed direct to Cordova, 140 miles up, where it was felt I would get the information I needed.

Out of Yakutat at 17:15, I took bearing on Cordova. From here on the weather was lovely. I climbed to 5,000 feet and flew direct, passing Yakataga 20 miles out from the mainland. The scenery was unparalleled. For years, my constant companion was a small automatic exposure camera I could use with one hand and I took several shots of the volcanic islands offshore. There had been a slight wind change that reduced the ground speed to 150 miles an hour which put us abeam Cordova at 18:30. I got on to the Cordova radio range, gave my position and intended destination and asked for any word on the condition of the runways or the harbour condition in case I had to make a water landing. Cordova's reply shook me. It had not been in contact with Anchorage since the quake. It had only sketchy information through Fairbanks. The Anchorage harbour was frozen. The runways were damaged excessively. The tower was out of commission and an aircraft on one of the runways was being used as a control centre. The operator had no weather dope.

Home never seemed further away as I acknowledged and advised I would attempt Anchorage but would return to Cordova if unable to land. Straight line air mileage from Cordova to Anchorage is 150 miles so I told Marquis I estimated Anchorage at 19:35. I crossed Prince William Sound, direct on course Portage at 5,000 feet, 80 miles west of Cordova.

My plan was to cross over Portage at the head of Cook Inlet and then begin the letdown into Anchorage 45 miles up the inlet. Passing over the saddle at the head of the inlet, then over Portage, I found myself on top of a cloud layer at 3,000 feet. I was unable to contact Portage and not yet able to raise Anchorage, although Cordova was still reading me five square. The ADF needle started swinging as I passed Portage but when tuned to Anchorage it just kept revolving. Then I tried the military field at Elmendorf but couldn't raise it, either. Despite the cloud I was able to follow the inlet by the surrounding peaks and could distinguish Mount McKinley, the highest point in North America, on the starboard.

The sun had set in a spectacular display of reds and oranges and the now black mountains were sharply silhouetted. I was getting edgy about the approaching darkness and worried about no weather or landing condition information at Anchorage. It was about then one eye began homing unconsciously to the fuel gauges. The ADF pointer swung suddenly while still on top of the cloud. I was able to pick up Anchorage and I called at once. They were faint and I was unable to read but they seemed to read me clearly as the response was immediate.

I calculated I was still 20 miles up inlet from Anchorage so I stayed on course watching for a break in the cloud cover. Six minutes later, I passed over Anchorage and watched the ADF reverse its heading. I was now at 2500 feet, just above the cloud and I called Anchorage again. This time, while indistinct, the operator was readable.

"Anchorage Control, this is Canadian Civil CF-OQA Super Grumman Goose. Do you read?"

"CF-OQA. Roger. Loud and clear."

"Anchorage, OQA. Request your weather and landing information."

Came the shocker:

"OQA, Anchorage. Runways unserviceable. What is your position,"

"Anchorage, OQA. 2500 on top, 2 miles southwest of the range station."

"OQA, Anchorage. Check your position. Confirm 2500."

"Anchorage, OQA. 2500 on top confirmed. Go ahead your weather."

"OQA, Anchorage. Our present weather, visibility one-eighth mile in light snow and fog. Wind, 270 degrees at 14. What is your destination?"

"Anchorage, OQA. Check your weather. My destination was to have been Anchorage. May I have a report on weather conditions for possible water landing?"

My passengers meanwhile were having fifteen fits. They were not concealing their frustration. I told them I would fly west out of Cook Inlet with the hope of finding a break in the cloud near the inlet's mouth and then would fly back under the cloud if water conditions and visibility permitted.

"OQA, Anchorage. Negative on the harbour. Repeat NEGATIVE on the harbour! Broken ice and thousands of gallons of jet fuel have spilled into the harbour from ruptured tanks."

"Anchorage, OQA. Roger. Check. All okay. Am returning Cordova. Please check me by Anchorage at 19:50. 3,000 feet climbing to 11,000 feet. Estimating Cordova at two zero five zero."

"Anchorage checks OQA. Have no contact with Cordova. Good luck captain."

My two passengers went back to the cabin, mad and glum. They seemed resigned to the fact they would not be in Anchorage this night. Darkness had come and I climbed to 11,000 feet, setting course for Cordova. A little while later Marquis leaned over my shoulder, peered into the blackness and in a voice no longer like a TV news announcer's, said: "Any idea where we are, Justin?" "Of course," I said, "estimating Cordova in 20 minutes."

As my normal flying was not done after dark, everything was unfamiliar. Even the instruments took on a strange dimension lighted by the panel bulbs. I could make out vague outlines of the mountains against the sky. Checking my charts, I was happy to find I had enough altitude to clear the peaks and ten minutes later I picked up the lights of Cordova and began descending.

"Cordova radio. This is Canadian Civil CF-OQA.

"OQA, Cordova."

"Cordova, OQA. Check me 15 miles west. 2500. Requesting runway lights and landing instructions."

"OQA, Cordova. Runway lights are on and you are cleared to land straight in from the west. We have no other reported traffic."

"Cordova, OQA. I am circling Cordova townsite. I do not have your runway lights in sight!"

"OQA, Cordova. Confirm 2,500 feet over Cordova."

"Affirmative."

"OQA, Cordova. There is a 3,000 foot ridge between Cordova and the airport. Recommend an additional 1,000 feet, captain."

He had told me just in time.

"Cordova, OQA. Roger. Check. All okay. Climbing to 3,500."

I climbed over the ridge two minutes later and 13 miles directly ahead was the beautiful sight of those runway lights. As I was beginning the pre-landing check Marquis was wiping the perspiration from his face. Landing was routine but while taxiing to the terminal building a profound weariness began to ache me.

Cordova radio checked me on at two zero zero five.

The flight from Prince Rupert had taken exactly 9 hours. Later, my log showed the flight to be 1200 miles, although the point to point from Rupert to Cordova is only 980 miles.

It was a chilly 30 degrees as we parked in front of the deserted terminal. I found a phone and called the tower to see about fuel and then a taxi into Cordova for the night. I found the phone lines all out and that the Cordova road had been badly mauled. There was an FM radio unit operating between the tower and the town and the tower said he would try to raise somebody in Cordova and call me back. Ten minutes later, the tower said a truck was on its way with six drums of fuel but it would take two hours.

The terminal was furnished with comfortable lounge chairs and the three of us passed out. A bit after 10 p.m., we wakened to the crashing of a tailgate and the dropping of gas drums. Outside there was an amiable gent who invited us to climb into the cab of his truck. It wasn't easy for Marquis has broad shoulders and so had the driver. McMinn and I are taller than average and with all the photographic equipment cases, it was to be no Sunday drive. The driver said: "call me Jack" and began a running commentary that lasted for the two solid hours it took to negotiate the road into town—and negotiate is the right word.

It is 13 miles from the airport to Cordova—a normal 15 minutes drive—but there are many bridges and the quake had collapsed them all. The road was torn in many places and deep crevices criss-crossed it. We were getting some awful bruises as we weaved about trying to find the best route. Crossing the bridges became a point of honour. They were at crazy angles that shifted us from one side of the cab to the other. All were broken in the middle so we had to climb the approach, descend the broken half, cross the creek and mud, climb the other half, then descend the far side approach to the road again, with more cracks and crevices until the next bridge.

Checking into the hotel and realizing we had eaten neither lunch nor dinner, we went across the street to the Pink Elephant. Over double orders of bacon and eggs and steaming coffee, we learned from the sheriff and others there had been little damage done in Cordova beyond the collapse of one house with a resulting death. The main concern was a tidal wave they felt was coming. Cordova is a deepsea port and when the tide receded the night of the quake it left the long docks high and dry. They had made up their minds the tide was soon to come rushing back to flood the town. Since there was still little communication, no one knew much about the surrounding communities.

We got back to the hotel at 2 a.m. and I asked the night clerk to wake me at five, forgetting that because of the time difference it would be actually 3 a.m., Alaska time. It seemed my eyes were closed only two seconds when there was a knock on the door. Jack was in the lobby waiting to take me to the airport to refuel and he had made arrangements for other transport to take my passengers two hours later.

I left the hotel, ropy from lack of sleep, and in the bitter cold darkness and light snow, the return trip was hell. It amazed me that even a four-wheel-drive vehicle was able to traverse such a mess. I was more aware of the damage as the crowded conditions of the inward trip had prevented me from seeing much. There were 13 bridges between Cordova and the airport and all of them were smashed. Jack was still chattering and I couldn't help feeling if he would only shut up we might have a better chance. At the field we set to the job of fuelling the Goose with a hand pump from the 45-gallon drums. When I think back now of the thousands of gallons I have pumped by hand! I was sweeping snow from the wings when Marquis and McMinn arrived.

Anchorage was now transmitting weather reports of zero zero visibility and light snow. No aircraft had landed there since the quake. Marquis was unhappy. I told him the weather outside Anchorage was good and suggested we could cover those areas first, hoping

Anchorage weather would improve later. He agreed and as the sun rose I took off from Cordova at 07:15.

Soon we were in brilliant sunshine and thrilling to the majesty of the snow-covered mountains. I could clearly make out Mount Goode in the west, over 10,000 feet high, and further to the north was the 12,000 foot peak of Mount Witherspoon. Our first point was to be Valdez, 50 miles northwest of Cordova at the head of a long narrow inlet. Long before reaching it we could see a pall of smoke rising high into the cold clear sky. McMinn, in the co-pilot's seat, was busy readying his camera. As we swept over the harbour we saw a litter of icebergs and debris of all description. In the middle there was a freighter anchored with part of a dock still hawsered to it. Oil coated the water and Valdez itself seemed levelled.

As I went low over the airport it was obvious the runway was unserviceable for wide cracks and crevices made it look like glass hit by a hammer. I circled the sad sight for a half hour while McMinn used up film getting fine newsreel coverage. The principal devastation was near the waterfront where several large oil storage tanks had toppled and were still burning. The fire had spread from building to building but was confined along the shoreline. There was extensive damage in the home areas and I saw several collapsed houses. I was flying low at 400 feet, and was having trouble manoeuvering the Goose within the narrow valley. As well, the smoke made for such restricted visibility I could catch only brief glimpses of the havoc below. Marquis wanted to land in the harbour to get some footage on the ground but that was impossible because of the condition of both water and runway.

We learned later that Valdez was only 30 miles

from the quake's epicentre while Anchorage was over 80 miles from it. McMinn said he was done and we left Valdez, to fly down the inlet. We crossed Prince William Sound again, to Whittier, a village of some 160 people. Again, storage tanks were on fire and the smoke was billowing. The settlement lies within a narrow inlet so I was forced to stay circling at 2,000 feet. The oily soot had settled on the snow of the mountains to turn it gray-black. McMinn shot away as we broke through the smoke periodically. Finally, both suggested we try for Anchorage again.

On the way, I flew over Portage, lower this time, and McMinn got excellent footage of the highway and railway that run from Anchorage to Whittier along the shore. Many of the bridges were completely destroyed and both road and rail were covered with long, deep stretches of avalanches and snowslides. Visibility was deteriorating again as I proceeded up the inlet. I was low, just above the ice.

Contacting Anchorage with more success than the night before, I was advised visibility was bad and still no aircraft had landed there. The operator said the runways were clear but the first 2,000 feet of the main runway was out of service. I was denied permission to land because of the lack of visibility.

I circled the outskirts of the battered city at three to four hundred feet altitude in moderate to heavy snow but only had quick glimpses of the downtown area. Back over the harbour, I could see at once it would be impossible to land because of the icebergs, debris and seeming millions of gallons of fuel covering the surface.

My passengers agreed there was only one thing to do—back to Cordova. On the way there was a weather phenomenon that left Prince William Sound with clear skies but the adjacent shores in heavy snow. Passing the uninhabited island of Montague I was amazed at the obvious raise of the terrain. The impression was the whole island had been tipped lengthways exposing a big area previously under water. This strip was free of snow and did not coincide with the high tide mark. I had been cruising well over three hours and I was thinking about the fuel shortage at Cordova. Cordova tower checked me on the runway at 10:40.

In the terminal, I learned the Pacific Northern Airlines agent was expecting an airliner soon that would continue on to Anchorage. Its radar would allow it to land at Anchorage where I had not been able. My passengers said they would take it if they could be guaranteed space out of Anchorage for Seattle that night and the PNA agent made the arrangements.

Then I became too generous for my own welfare. I gave my remaining cash to Marquis because I knew he would need at least some funds for the rest of the way to Vancouver, but it left me without a cent. Much later, Marquis told me he signed checks for those two days worth over $3,000.

I wished them luck, saw them aboard the PNA Constellation and returned to hand-pumping the last of the fuel out of Talkative Jack's drums. I calculated I had enough to reach Yakutat where, hopefully, I could refuel. I had to keep going for I was determined I was going to keep my scheduled run out of Prince Rupert to the Queen Charlottes next morning.

I departed Cordova at exactly noon for the long, lonely journey home and it wasn't to be easy.

Just as I lost sight of Cordova, I flew into moderate to heavy snow forcing me to follow the shore all the way down the coast at between 50 and 100 feet above the water. In particular, I recall crossing Yakutat Bay, abandoning the shore just once. Tuning the ADF to Yakutat, I flew 20 miles across the bay right down in heavy snow. I was timing this part and was veering to the south of Yakutat to avoid coming up on the shore-line and not have time to avoid flying into the harbour with possible disastrous results. I was abeam Yakutat when the needle swung but I couldn't see the shore. I called the tower there and heard the old, chilling story: "Zero, zero, in heavy snow." As many times as I have heard that phrase I have never become used to it. Quickly calculating the distance to Juneau, I acknowledged and advised I was on course Juneau, with the alternative of Sitka. That was the second time I was signed off with: "Good luck, captain!" This time, I thought: "I'm going to need it". From here on I knew the problem would be shortage of fuel.

The weather was frightful from Yakutat to Cape Spencer. It was 200 miles around by the shoreline and all I could see in endless monotony, when I could see, was the desolate beach with its edging of stunted, wind-swept forest and the eternal Pacific breakers, mile after mile after mile. Even passing Lituya Bay and the Fair-weather glacier didn't relieve the monotony. Eighty-five minutes beyond Yakutat, I roared over the lonely wire-less station at the Cape which is nothing more than a rock promontory pounded by the Pacific. I had not been above 200 feet since departing Cordova and as I entered Cross Sound with but 34 miles to Juneau the needles of the fuel gauges were bouncing against the empty marks. I was down to the fumes when, skimming over the trees on the north end of Admiralty Island, I made a routine water landing at 14:40.

The dock attendant made the Goose fast and put a small fender under the wingfloat to prevent it bouncing against the decking. A realization of utter fatigue took over. I had been flying for almost 28 hours with only two hours sleep and I had eaten only one meal. I asked the attendant to fuel up and check the oil and then wearily made my way up the rainy dock to the office of Alaska Coastal-Ellis Airlines.

I had already decided to try to clear Customs here at Juneau which would allow me to go on non-stop to Prince Rupert. If I was to get there before dark, time was now all-important. The agent called Customs and was told someone would be right down. Thirty minutes went by while I fretted and sipped coffee. I called Customs this time, forgetting in my half-awake state that this was Easter Sunday for it seemed a week since Good Friday. A bored voice said it had received the message and would be along presently. Attempting politeness, I explained I was a commercial pilot and it was imperative I reach Rupert before dark. Click. The son of a gun hung up.

A man came in a business suit twenty minutes later and said he was the Customs agent. I gave him my manifest and custom's documents and once again explained time was running out. I have completed Customs procedures in minutes hundreds of times but this was to be the time things were to be different.

The questions that character thought up to ask! Did I clear Customs at Juneau? (It said so on my manifest.) Did I make any other landings? Why didn't I land at Anchorage? Why was I clearing Customs at Juneau instead of Ketchikan? Why did I go to Anchorage? Where were my two passengers? By what authority did I leave them at Cordova? Was I aware this was

Easter Sunday?

None of my answers satisfied him and like a Hollywood trial lawyer, started questioning all over again, trying to trap me into different answers. I was flaming and I cut him short. "We've covered it all," I said, "I can answer no other way. I insist you stamp my documents and allow me to proceed."

I was up the creek good now. He was apoplectic. I couldn't help noticing over his shoulder, the Coastal-Ellis agent was shaking his head in utter disbelief at his behaviour. The character spun, stabbed some paper from the counter and waved it under my nose. "You go over to that table," he yelled, "and write a full report of your activities since entering Alaska!" You proper son of a bitch, I thought.

I went because I had to and I began scribbling furiously while he leaned on the coffee machine and watched me with a smirk. He came and leaned over my shoulder. "It had better be readable," he said, "or you can damn well do it again."

Trembling with anger, I was appealing such treatment when he bent down nose to nose and stared in my eyes. "Complete the report," he hissed, "or I'll impound the aircraft. Suit yourself."

I completed it. I thrust it at him and strode to the window to keep my hands from him. He began reading slowly and I could swear he moved his lips. Every so often he would ask why I had done this or that. When he finished he said: "Okay, you're clear to go," and added, "as soon as you have paid the Customs fee of $73.16.".

"What?" I exploded. "The usual fee is five dollars!"

"Not today it isn't buddy. It's a holiday. You can

take it or leave it."

I told him I didn't have a dime; I had given all the cash I had to my passengers. Would he take a check? No, he wouldn't take a check. But look at all these credit cards. How did he know they weren't phoney? Would he bill my company? No, he wouldn't bill my company.

I was about to jump the bastard when the Coastal-Ellis agent came to the rescue. He said he would pay the fee and I could repay his agent in Rupert. No, he wouldn't accept that. There was more haggling until he gave in grudgingly by slowly taking out a small stamp pad and a stamp and began stamping and initialling my documents.

I went down the ramp to the float at a dead run and I was releasing the mooring ropes when I turned around and there he was again.

He had no right to do it, but he insisted on searching the aircraft. More minutes flew by until he reappeared in the cabin door. As he jumped to the dock he said, "Okay, sonny, on your way."

Just once in a man's lifetime he meets another he knows he will never forget and he hopes just once he will meet again up a dark alley.

The remainder of the downward leg was routine. I went out of the water and up the Prince Rupert ramp at 18:45. It was just dark.

If this story has an ending it lies with Marquis and McMinn who captured a rare newsbreak and provided the world with the first films of the earthquake's aftermath. It broke coast to coast on Canadian and U.S. television on the late Sunday night news.

"Thar She Blows"

"THAR SHE BLOWS, 500 yards to the starboard!" The whalers' old crowsnest cry sounded strange in the cockpit. It came from one of seven whalehunters who were aboard my twin engine flying boat, 300 feet above the gray Pacific combers, 140 miles southwest of Vancouver Island's northern tip. It was my first aerial whalehunt over the open sea and it was an exciting experience.

There had been a few days to prepare for the charter and a few hours to bone up on whaling because all I knew of it was a boyhood memory of Captain Ahab chasing Moby Dick.

I found that New Bedford whalers, sailing around Cape Horn, spent three or four years in the water off the North Pacific coast before returning home and in the bay at Anacortes in Puget Sound, they had built a whaling station about 1840. The New Englanders hunted the B.C. coast from 1820 to 1860, when the American Civil War began. Up to the introduction of kerosene in 1852, whale oil was a main source of illumination, other than wax or tallow candles. The baleen, the flexible, bony strainers in the mouth, was cut away for the making of combs and corset stays, but the rest of the whale was boiled down to oil and it was the number of barrels of oil returned to the New England docks that marked the success of a whaling voyage.

About 1910, there were three main whaling stations on the British Columbia coast—Kyuoquot on the west coast of Vancouver Island, Naden Harbour and Rose Harbour on the north and south ends of the Queen Charlottes. They operated until about 1920 and after that there was no whale hunting until the 1940's when B.C. Packers Ltd. turned the old Coal Harbour wartime seaplane patrol base on the Island into a station and began operations with modern catcher boats and processing equipment.

Latterly, in partnership with a Japanese company, B.C. Packers seasonal catch from May to September has averaged about 700 whales but it has run into severe competition from large Japanese and Russian fleets each complete with factory ship, catcher boats, fresh water boat and maintenance tugs, all operating in international water beyond the 12-mile limit. The slaughter of whales has been so heavy it is feared certain species will soon be extinct.

Six catcher boats are based at Coal Harbour, most skippered by Scandinavian captains. They all employ the exploding harpoon fired from a foredeck cannon—a humane weapon because it causes instant death. Air is pumped into the carcass and marked with a buoy and light to be picked up an hour or day later when the ship has enough kill to return to the station.

There are 21 species of whales on the coast and the humpback, sei, sperm, blue and fin varieties range in length from 40 to 110 feet. I checked one season's catch of the six boats operating in an area of 160 to 200 miles around the mouth of Quatsino Sound, Vancouver Island, and found 342 sei, 169 sperm, 156 fin, 28 blue, 17 humpback and one baird-peak were captured.

The sight at the station is bloody and only for the strong of stomach. A power winch drags the blue-black beast out of the water tail first and up the red-slick ramp where formerly Canso patrol flying boats waddled home. The crater in the skin, marking where the harpoon entered and exploded, looks no larger than a mosquito welt in contrast to the mammal's size. Young men, a number of them university students acquiring the fees for another year's study, wearing sharp-nailed boots against slipping, attack the carcass with long flensing knives. They are honed to a razor edge and the 18-inch thick outer blubber falls away like soft white soap. Large hooks attached to the steel cable of the winch peel back the blubber strips in sections as the flensers cut them free. As each long strip leaves the carcass, another winch drags it up another ramp into one of the two old hangars. There, men cut the fat into chunks and push them into a floor opening feeding the boiling vats below.

The red, succulent meat lies in two long loins under the blubber. If the meat comes from an edible specie an international process begins. Working in the other hangar is a precision-team of Japanese nationals. These men are professionals in whale meat rendering.

They have worked in the Antarctic on Japanese factory ships and all over the world where Japan has sent its whaling fleets. Through special immigration permit, they come into the country as a team, stay within the Coal Harbour station, and leave for home at the end of the season still a team. Wearing the forage caps and tucked-in pants of national custom, they look like extras in an old wartime movie of the Pacific theatre.

Japan and Russia particularly, are protein-poor countries. To satisfy the lack, their fleets scour the world for varieties of fish that North Americans will not eat. These are ground-fish, to give them a broad name, and the meat is usually coarse. The Japanese and Russians consider anything from the sea edible and a morning spent in the Tokyo wholesale fish market is proof of this. There are stringent controls, and one is to ensure the meat at the cutting end has been inspected, properly rendered and bacteria-protected—thus, this team on faraway Vancouver Island preparing whale meat for their countrymen.

The little men cut the loins into large chunks and shove them into vats of fresh water and other baths before the big pieces reach the cutting tables where others slice them into exactly-sized 40-pounds blocks. These are wrapped, sealed and flash frozen. The meat becomes rock hard less than an hour after being cut from the carcass.

Meat considered not fit for human consumption is shipped frozen to pet food manufacturers as far as California. The head, tail, bones and viscera are cooked and the fine solids are made into meals. The liquid, high in protein, hormones and B12 vitamin, is shipped in tank cars across Canada for feed companies to mix with plant nutrients. The liver and its valuable vitamin A is processed mainly for pharmaceutical companies. The oils, fractionated into many grades, become necessary ingredients of lipsticks, paints, plastics and at least 500 commercial products. It is used as an exotic lubricant for fine machinery. Occasionally, the flensers will find a chunk of ambergris in the stomach that might weigh 200 pounds. This is sold at high price to French perfume manufacturers who require it as the only fixative possible for their expensive varieties. Nothing is wasted One of nature's most magnificent mammals does not die uselessly.

Now you must re-read this in the past tense. Early in 1968, B.C. Packers Ltd. was forced to the decision to close the Coal Harbour station because of the depletion of the whales. Thus, for Canada at least, an age-old story of Pacific northwest whaling has ended for perhaps a long time and my yarn of an aerial whale hunt has become a story of "the good old days."

. . . . So there I was at 0900 hours, landing in a sheltered cove off the mouth of Quatsino Sound near the northwest tip of Vancouver Island, after locating the whaling ship *West Whale I* anchored tight against the rough rock bluff of Restless Bite.

In making arrangements for the search it had been emphasized that the morning sun or late evening sun were the best conditions to see the whale spouts. They stand out better in a slanting light just as sun through a waterfall at a low angle picks up the highlights. If nothing else we are weather-wise on this coast for the elements are on constant alert to maul the unwary. There was a chance of evening fog at that time of year so we chose the morning in the hope of having the hunt completed before noon. This was the second consecutive day the flight had been delayed for lack of ideal conditions. Then had come my go-ahead at 0800 hours.

West Whale I, was one of a fleet of five whalers in service this September morning. She was a gray-rust-yeeuuch following a long busy season in coast water. She blended into the granite backdrop and was almost invisible.

As I taxied my fuel-heavy flying boat to within hailing distance of the whaler my mind was a jumble: how far out in the Pacific would they want me to go? What was the weather like out there? If I had an engine failure how would the crate perform on one engine with this heavy fuel load as I was up to the gas caps with 200 gallons to see me through four hours of low altitude cruising with a half hour reserve. The weather ship at Station "Papa", located 300 miles out in the Pacific and 200 miles northwest of our area, had been reporting intermittent broken ceilings with gradual improvement expected through the day, but with occasional rain showers and a southwest wind of 20 knots. I hadn't yet been told my flight pattern but from discussions during the arrangements I knew the ships were ranging 200 miles out from Vancouver Island.

As I cut the engines, a power launch from the whaler was coming alongside with seven passengers. Captain Christophersen introduced himself and I helped him climb into the cabin. He was in his late sixties, six feet two, with piercing blue eyes framed in a weathered face that took in everything. With him were six tanned seamen and each carried a three-foot stick with a clamp at one end. I found out later they used them as monopods for their binoculars which at the moment swung from their shoulders in battered cases.

After the launch moved off I closed the hatch and

as I went forward to the cockpit I was assailed by the smell of oilskins impregnated with whale oil, salt water and sweat. It filled the cabin. "That, by God," I thought "is the real smell of working seamen."

The captain had made himself at home in the co-pilot's seat. He had a metal clamp board on his knees holding a white sheet of paper ruled in half-inch squares. There were circles here and there and he said those were the other *West Whalers, II, III, IV* and *V*. Then he put an acetate sheet over the grid and began blue-pencilling straight lines between the other whalers. Using a parallel rule, a compass and a protractor he wrote in the magnetic compass headings corresponding to each line.

"We will make for *West Whale IV*," he said. "She is sailing southward and should be about here." He pointed to the ship's position on the grid and drew a blue line to that spot. "After picking her up." he continued, "we will cruise on a series of separate headings between the different whalers. I want you to maintain an approximate 300 feet altitude. It is the ideal height for spotting spouts. I suggest you give me your estimated ground speed on each of the separate headings and keep track of the minutes flown on each."

Off the water and headed for the flat horizon, he gave me a heading of 195 degrees magnetic he estimated would put us over *West Whale IV*. There was a headwind of 20 knots. I calculated my ground speed at 130 knots and advised the captain. He nodded. Meanwhile he had tuned the auxiliary radio to his company frequency and using the headset, was talking to his ship in Norwegian. As I held the course, I glanced back periodically at the gradually disappearing shoreline. Forty minutes later it dropped below the horizon and for the first time in my years of flying the coast I had nothing but open sea around me. What a consolation was the needle of the automatic direction finder pointing the reciprocal heading back to my base at Port Hardy.

The rolling swells were thirty to forty feet high, two hundred yards apart. The wind was picking up and was whipping the wavetops into spindrift that went skimming down the leaside of the swells giving the sea a fascinating, light and dark, criss-cross pattern. There was a curious hypnotic effect to the scene and it required concentration to keep my attention focused on the compass.

I advised the captain of our reduced ground speed and he gave me a new heading of 193 degrees magnetic. Forty-five minutes after takeoff, he leaned across to say the ship should be directly ahead and even as he said it, there she was. She was only a distant speck that vanished, then reappeared, then vanished again in the heavy swell. The captain focused his glasses, nodded and grunted—a man of few words. We closed rapidly and three or four minutes later we were circling her low, a 100 feet above the crests. What a little thing she was to be so far out at sea as she rolled and pitched like a cork in a cup. As we circled I could see the crowsnest lookout waving as were the crew from the deck. She was on a southerly heading and although she appeared stationary she was cruising at 7 knots.

The captain gave me a new heading of 182 degrees magnetic, in a southerly direction. When I told him our ground speed was approximately 130 knots he began laying out the new heading on his overlay. Leaving *West Whale IV* behind, I maintained course and tuned into Comox radio range on my HF, picked up the definite audio A, *di-dah, di-dah* which indicated I was approaching the southwest leg of the Comox radio range station. It gave me some assurance in the unfamiliar seascape. We cruised this course until we crossed the range leg, putting us directly seaward of the airbase at Tofino. Our distance from shore was unknown but I estimated it at 100 miles. I wasn't to see land for another three hours.

After crossing the radio range leg, I began picking the audio N, *dah-di, dah-di* and using my air charts pointed this out to the captain. He just nodded. He gave me the impression he was aware of our position at all times and I had the feeling my knowledge of navigation was not required. At this time he came up with a new heading of 275 degrees magnetic and said: *West Whale II* is dead ahead." He asked my estimated wind drift that I figured was about 5 degrees to starboard and he nodded and said: "Just maintain your course, captain, the 'Two' should be forty minutes ahead."

At a point southwest of "Four", that we had passed and circled earlier, the cry "thar she blows, 500 yards to the starboard" came floating from the cabin above the radio static in my headphones. I veered in that direction and began to circle. There wasn't one whale, there were three. Those silver-black submarine shapes seemed gigantic to my untrained eye. Christopherson grunted. "Not bad," he said, "two twenty tonners probably, and one forty tonner. We'll get them." Then he radioed their position to *West Whale IV* and told me to continue on line for the "Two". "Poor whales," I thought, "your time has come."

All doubts I might have had were dispelled for the remainder of the search. He was a master mariner who knew where he was all the time and he would have complete control of any situation. Periodically, I would glance at the Port-Hardy-pointing needle of the ADF but it was only habit. I relaxed knowing I need only hold my headings, watch my flying time and check my fuel consumption.

West Whale II was just where the captain said she would be and we circled her once. We then took up three more headings and worked our way, zig-zag, between the sister ships, "Three" and "Five". We had just passed the "Five" and were about five miles off her stern when we came over another whale. It was a big one. Sixty to seventy tons, said the captain, about 70 to 80 feet long. While her position was being radioed to the "Five", I kept circling and watching a great spray geysering from her blowhole. A whale is a magnificent mammal.

The weather was deteriorating. The ceilings had dropped appreciably and the weathership's predicted rain squalls were becoming prevalent. There had been several squalls when we lost sight of everything around us but the chilly water below. The captain was getting discouraged and I was beginning to glance frequently at the dropping fuel gauges. The hours of low altitude, compass watching and inability to see land had made me tense and when the captain tapped my elbow and said: "Take her in, skipper, we've done well for the day," I veered the aircraft about with unseemly haste. I double checked my heading on Port Hardy on the ADF and setting a course allowing for drift, settled back for a 30-minute flight to Restless Bite.

As he descended into his launch beside the *West Whale I*, the captain paused on the step: "Thank you, skipper," he grinned, "it was a satisfactory hunt and I am confident the ships will pick up the whales we spotted." Then he added: "May be $70,000 in that lot!"

I shut the hatch and took off for the Port Hardy base. "Nice percentage," I thought to myself, "Seventy thousand bucks for a $500 charter!"

Stuck in the Mud

HOW MANY TIMES have you driven your car with the emergency brake on, or forgotten to switch off your headlights after emerging from a tunnel, or got your hands crossed and did the opposite of your intention— stupid things to make you wonder if you're slipping?

I have had my share of stupidities too—all minor thank God, otherwise you wouldn't be reading this now. It is redundant to say that a major stupidity committed while piloting an aircraft is likely to be the last the pilot will make. Running out of fuel, landing with the wheels up, water landing on pontoons with the wheels down, are the kind of major pilot errors that provide headlines. Luckily I have had none of those— but the silly sort, the no-consequence kind, the sort we call "finger trouble", of these I have had my share.

I had been flying amphibian seaplanes out of Port Hardy on Vancouver Island's eastern coast for almost a year. During a three-week stretch, I had been using a Cessna 180 exclusively with no flight time on the Beavers. With the busy season coming, another pilot was posted to the base who had a lot of experience on Beavers but had never been checked out on amphibian Beavers. It was my job to take him up and instruct him on the use of the amphibious undercarriage, specially the doublecheck system we had for making sure the gear was up or down when landing on water or runway.

It was my first time in a Beaver for almost a month and my takeoff check was more thorough than usual as I reacquainted myself with the now-slightly unfamiliar instruments and controls. Airborne, I watched my student begin to pump up the undercart which requires changing a lever to the "up" position and then pumping a handle. Throttling back from takeoff power, I automatically set the engine instruments for the cruise settings of a Cessna instead of a Beaver.

We lumbered across Johnstone Strait at less than 100 miles an hour, rather than the Beaver's cruising speed of 110 or 115 mph. I was at a complete loss as I checked the settings and the fuel. Everything was as it should be, so why the poor performance? The student was looking quizzically from the gauges to me and back again. I made a routine landing on a mainland inlet and taxiing back and forth, pumping the gear up and down, I showed him how the retractable wheels could be used for slowing down or when approaching a dock in a wind. We decided he would fly us back to the base. He made a lovely takeoff and there we were cruising across the Strait at the correct 115 mph. Then I realized my goof. He never mentioned it then or afterward but it still is an embarrassing moment to me.

A Beaver carries three belly fuel tanks and a pilot has to switch manually from the forward to the centre and finally to the stern tank as fuel is consumed. It is an old point of pride with any Beaver pilot to make the change from an empty tank to a full one at the last second without stalling the engine. Unlike an automobile engine, when a Beaver engine runs out of gas, it stops. No cough, no sputter, no warning, you're dead. It can scare the hell out of you if your mind has been on something else and you have failed to notice the gauge nearing the "empty" mark or the dropping fuel pressure.

The passengers grab the arm rests and you feel their eyes boring into your neck while you are scrambling for the fuel selector valve, switching to another tank, wobbling up the pressure on the hand-operated wobble pump, at the same time easing the throttle so when the fuel starts flowing it won't pour in and stop the engine again. It's called "blowing a tank" and there isn't a pilot of small aircraft living who hasn't been embarrassed by it.

Most of the logging camp docks are murder. For most of them, "dock" is too generous. Many are nothing but a sixty-foot log sticking out from the shore. Every time you come up to one you meet a different set of circumstances and each one has to be taken *now*, as it comes. If the tide is running out, there is an eddy in front. If it is running in, there is a pileup of water against the face you are approaching. If you misjudge the current and the wind as you cut the engine, you find yourself continuing merrily at the same speed and clobbering the dock/barge/log/landing with the nose of the pontoon hard enough to bend it. We hate bending airplanes.

A Beaver dead on the water, has great windage and moves like a sailboat in a hurricane, or so it seems. There you are in the pilot's seat and there's that dock float thirty feet long and only as big as the airplane itself, coming at you fast. The tide is strong with you and wind gusts your tail. You're alone. You can't go into reverse like a boat. Your approach angle is all wrong and instead of gliding alongside you know you're going to prang. You wrench open the door, jump down to the pontoon and from there to the dock, hoping you don't break a leg, grab a strut, dig in and hold on. Your nice, light, airy Beaver, so maneuverable in the air, is now a weighty clot with her mind bent on self-destruction. Many a passenger has earned his flight by grabbing hold and tieing her down. Those times are embarrassing too.

Along most areas of the coast the tide rises and falls an average twelve to fourteen feet every day and a pilot has to have with him as many hydrographic charts and tide books as a sea pilot. Misjudging the tide, the locale and type of beach can add up to embarrassment.

I remember an incident when I nosed the aircraft up to a sandy beach while a passenger ran up to inspect quickly some machinery at an abandoned quartz mine. He said he would be only five minutes so I tied down to a boulder with a long rope. As the tide receded I kept nudging the ship back, barely afloat, but as 15 minutes went by I pushed her well out, moved the boulder to the water's edge and ran to the mine to hurry him along. We got into a discussion and another 15 minutes flew past before we arrived back on the beach on the run to find her high and dry on the sand.

Night was coming on as we strolled down the beach about four miles to a fisherman's cabin, there to spend the night with him. I remember my passenger kicking the drift wood disconsolately, saying: "The damnable part is my wife will think I'm spending the night in a Vancouver nightclub." The tide was full at 3 a.m. and the fisherman boated us back to the aircraft in the rain. Following his stern light, I taxied the ship back to his mooring and returned to a firelit bunk. It was a stupid incident, annoying to my passenger, embarrassing to me.

I was really red-faced when Gordon Best, the former general manager, paid Prince Rupert one of his routine inspection visits and as was his custom, came to the house for the evening. A great sports fisherman, he rarely finds time for it but he always enjoys talking about it. After dinner, I set up the projector and some trays of slides to show him my views of good fishing spots and catches. They were nicely sequenced, one shot leading to the next, when at the flick of the switch, there in all its infamy was the beginning of a sequence I had forgotten about—blown up 15 feet square—in vivid color, a magnificently exposed scene of my red and white Grumman Goose up to its axles in mud. "Oops," I said, and flicked the switch again to bring up yet another view of the same sad sight. "Hold it right there," the boss said, "where and what the hell is that all about?" This is the story I had to tell him.

The company has a generous provision allowing pilots private use of aircraft if the privilege is not abused. It asks only a nominal rate in return. At Prince Rupert where I was based as the lone company pilot, I flew when I had to, which seemed eternally, and when a rare spare hour showed up I made the most of the policy and took off for a remote lake to try to bring back a couple of fish for dinner. Union Lake was my favorite, about a 10-minute flight from the base. Its rainbow trout are fat, fighting and fast. The occasions were rare and came up quickly. It was only a matter of a phone call any time to my fishing buddy, Walter Wainman, and we would be airborne.

The story of the mud-stranded Goose began one Saturday afternoon late in February when Walt phoned wondering if the lake was ice-free yet. When I said I hadn't been over it in a long time he suggested we go and look and as it happened I was free. An hour later three of us were on our way. Walt had brought Gene, a Vancouver friend. Union Lake's setting is superb. Long and narrow, the sliver of water nestles between high, snowy peaks more picturesque than a postcard. It is only 1½ miles long and three to five hundred yards wide. As we circled above it we were disappointed to find it still frozen over except for a small bit at the end where the lake emptied into a stream that ran a crooked course down to Union Inlet.

Our first thought was to return to base but then we decided to land in the inlet, moor, and try casting upstream. I went around again and found a small sand beach close to where the stream entered the inlet. The water was like glass as I made a long, low approach and taxied slowly to the beach. The water was clear and instead of sand I could see now the beach was fine shale. Putting the wheels down, I taxied up the slight slope out of the water and turned the Goose around to face the inlet. It wasn't until then I checked the tide book against the clock and found the tide falling. I'll take a look at that beach again, I thought. At the shoreline there seemed to be a long dropoff and a short piece out, the water seemed at least 15 feet deep. Good enough for an hour, I said to myself, and picking up my waders and gear headed up the beach to the mouth of the stream to find Walt and Gene. Upstream, we fished the better part of an hour and a half then with not a bite, we dejectedly headed back. Putting our gear aboard, I walked over to the dropoff again and while there was still a gradual slope, the water didn't seem to be as deep as I had first thought, allowing for the tide fall. I taxied down the shale into the water and was only about ten feet out when I knew I had a problem. The Goose was still on the bottom and I was requiring more power as I was nowhere near floating. I was in less than two feet of water. I managed to force her another five or six feet until the ship stuck hard in the mud-shale with the tide still receding. There was nothing to do but wait.

I switched on the radio and advised the base I had a minor difficulty and would stay overnight in Union Inlet. It was a simple message, acknowledged. I didn't elaborate because news travels fast on the bush network and I didn't want repercussions. I said I would return first thing next morning. Soon we were in the middle of a large mud flat and we were able to climb out. The nice clean Goose was up to its axles and its fat keel was flat on the beach.

I never saw two more jubilant guys. Finding themselves stranded in a rugged fastness of the north Pacific coast was a hell of an adventure—something to tell the boys. Wait, I thought, this is February, and it is going to get damn cold tonight. I knew too when the tide came in around one o'clock in the morning, I would have to taxi the ship and find a mooring for the rest of the night. We made a fire from drift wood and we cooked one small piece of garlic sausage that for some strange reason had been aboard. We weren't concerned about food as there were two ration kits and each is sufficient for six people from four to six days. There were only six cigarettes though and that was the worst part.

We spent a long time trying vainly to dig a path out to the water just for something to do. We used poles and sticks and the ship's paddle to dig a couple of trenches and we put some driftwood planks under the wheels. The two boys hung on to the tail struts as I revved up the engines and tried to break loose. I gave her a burst but she was weighted too deep and wouldn't budge. When I looked around, the two of them were black with mud thrown by the propellor wash and they were in hysterics. What an adventure! Some people have a queer sense of humor.

By six o'clock it was black and the northern chill started to grab us. The tide turned at nine o'clock and we watched the water creep back toward the Goose. We climbed aboard at 10 o'clock to sit in the blackness waiting for the aircraft to float free. That happened at midnight. Using the wing landing lights, I taxied down the inlet to a log boom I had noticed when we were first landing, and tieing up, prepared to put in a long, cold night. A floating Goose sits low in the water and your feet are actually below the water line. We damn near froze for we had only sweaters, light jackets and slacks. The heaters were dead since they depend on the slip stream and the engines operating. Walter was trying to sleep kneeling, his knees on one side and his arms and forehead on the seat across the aisle. I have long legs and I was stretched across a seat with my feet up into the cockpit across the sill through the door. I don't think I slept a full five minutes the whole night. Gene, the nut, spent the night sitting in the rear seat with the hatch partially open, dangling a fishing line.

He looked as if he couldn't be happier.

Dawn came at seven a.m. to find three cold, hungry, dirty, disillusioned fishermen. Fifteen minutes later we were back at Prince Rupert and the bacon and eggs tasted like manna that morning.

The boss sat through my long tale with a stern face. When I finished there was a long silence and I thought I was going to get it for sure. He watched my concern for a few minutes and then began to laugh. I could see the fisherman in him seeing the funny side and that he had finally caught me with my pants down.

All he said was not to attempt the mud flat again and I didn't.

I Take
a Short Cut

OVER THE YEARS a commercial aircraft pilot acquires a special wisdom concerning his particular kind of flying that along with basic common sense enables him to survive and helps assure the welfare of his passengers and his aircraft. It is not something he learns overnight or from books. It takes long experience to teach him all he must know and it is the many encounters with fate he is certain to have that will prove his best teacher.

A captain who flies continental and inter-continental aircraft operates by rules called Instrument Flight Regulations. They are referred to as "IFR" and the procedures are specialized. He must know a collection of facts about high altitude flying, icing conditions, instrument regulations and rules for route flying, instrument landings, holding patterns and many other procedures.

My kind of flying is controlled by Visual Flight

Regulations, called "VFR". They require the same thorough knowledge of an aircraft but a completely different knowledge of flight procedures. The basic rules are the same, particularly at major airports or in areas where there is a high concentration of air traffic, but there the similarity ends. I must operate my aircraft in much the same way an IFR captain does but I have to rely on my eyes and ears to a greater degree. He flies a straight line as much as possible, from point to point and sometimes he is in zero visibility for the entire route. I cannot do this. The area I fly must be as familiar to me as my garden.

My area was the coastline of British Columbia and I had to know every turn of the waterways forming the complicated network of islands and channels; the queer landmarks, like a great crooked fir tree with a broken top I remember that angles from a cliff. There is a branch dangling toward the water like a scarecrow's arm, and most always a bald-headed eagle is perched on it, watching for fish. This is one facet. Each season has its own peculiar weather conditions and a lot of my area has little or no communication about up-to-the-minute conditions. I had to make decisions based on what I saw and heard. A crackle in my headphones could be lightning, approaching snow or heavy rain. In poor visibility when flying low on the water, you can hear a fishboat ahead by the putt-putt radio static from its engine generator, or a tug by its steady diesel-caused hum, or a coastal freighter with its resonant growl that comes not only from its engines but from its propellor and driveshaft.

The weather is one of the most challenging and fascinating aspects of flying the coast. Beautiful summer days when flying should be a delight, can still hold conditions as dangerous as the winter months with their gales, snow storms, low level ice and bad visibility. The fleecy balls of fluff that look lovely on color film as they float in a blue sky are in reality, powerhouses of energy and potential disaster. I never saw the centre of one and I never wanted to. I will never forget flying between, around, over and under them, enthralled with their massive beauty, but my fear of what they might hold never lessened.

The small airline companies frown on the old phrase: "seat of the pants flying", and I suppose they are right. It is a bad phrase when applied to the context of public image and a company's responsibility to its passengers. But in another way, a VFR pilot does fly by the seat of his pants, which really means all his senses are alert to every detail of the terrain and every caprice of nature. Like an Indian tracker in the bush, his keen, trained senses are as necessary as his panel instruments.

The gradual accumulation of information as I have indicated, and the development of the inner senses to a point that recognition of a warning is automatic, finally develops a formidable line within the experienced VFR pilot and he never crosses that line for it becomes his standard and his basis for survival. In a lesser way he is like the overcautious driver who never exceeds 30 miles an hour; the skin diver who won't submerge below 25 feet; the cruiser owner who won't leave the dock if the wind is above 15 knots. These also are intangible base lines of survival.

At the same time, to those people and to professional pilots, there comes at least once when an unrecognized force takes charge and despite all the accumulated wisdom to the contrary, they barrel ahead anyway. Perhaps they are caught in a set of circumstances and the only route to survival is on the other side of their self-set "line". If they are lucky, they have something to talk about in the locker room. If they aren't, they become statistics and short items for tomorrow's papers.

Now I want to tell you about the one day when I crossed *my* line.

The winds during the night had been gale force and by a unique meteorological freak that occurs around Prince Rupert when the wind is from certain directions, visibility was zero. The morning wasn't much better but the forecast called for general improvement as the day progressed and as the system moved east.

After three one-hour delays and with scant en route weather information, I took off from Rupert at 11:00 on my regular scheduled flight to Ocean Falls and Port Hardy, with the normal en route stops. There were no passengers but I had considerable freight. There was a 450-pound bundle of gillnetting for Butedale and another for Bella Bella. For Klemtu there was a crankshaft for a fishboat and a small quantity of groceries. On a previous trip into Bella Bella, Mrs. Williams had given me $15 and a list of things she needed for her daughter's birthday party. I had these things in a box along with another containing the child's party dress from Simpson-Sears.

The weather was not good. It was extremely gusty. There was poor visibility and there were periods of heavy rain squalls when it was reduced to near zero.

I made several attempts to land at Butedale, a tiny fishing village in Graham Reach, but gave it up because of the rough water and the strong gusts. I advised the agent there that, unable to land, I was proceeding to Klemtu but I would stop there on the return flight if the weather improved. At Klemtu, 40 miles south and further down the channel, despite its sheltered location, extreme turbulence again prevented a landing. The wind was curling over the ridge and hitting the water with great force, then fanning out in all directions. Trying to contact the agent there without success, I proceeded southeast another 30 miles to Bella Bella. The weather was better and I made a routine landing and disembarked my freight. Mrs. Williams said she liked the party dress. I picked up five passengers and once airborne for Ocean Falls I could see the ceiling definitely lifting in the west and the sky brightening out in the Pacific. I flew up Gunboat Passage into Fisher Channel and then into Cousins Inlet. There was a strong inflow but visibility was good. The landing was routine but bumpy for Ocean Falls can be tricky.

In the office at the top of the ramp, over some coffee, the agent, Red Reiffer, always had ready, he told me the Vancouver Island weather was bad and he had cancelled the southern part of the flight to Port Hardy. It appeared I would be returning to Rupert without passengers unless I could get down at Klemtu and Butedale on the way. He said there were three passengers at Klemtu and two at Butedale waiting to go to Rupert. I finished my coffee, picked up the manifest and Red and I went out to put some fuel in the ship.

I gave the Goose its customary external check, the tail surface, the rudder, flaps, undercarriage and both engines and I even checked the drain plugs in the hull. When I climbed aboard Red pulled away the steps, and with a wave to him, I fired up, went through a normal runup, checked the instruments and taxied down the ramp into the saltchuck. I retracted the wheels at once and with engine temperatures reading normal, made an immediate takeoff into the wind.

The ceiling had lifted considerably. In calculating quickly the flight time to Prince Rupert, with the restriction that my before-dark grounding time there had to be 16:25 or before, I knew I had no time to spare.

Veering sharp to starboard, I climbed out over the twin lakes, taking a short cut we call "the back way". I advised Ocean Falls of my time off and that I was proceeding to Klemtu and Butedale direct. When I had reached 2,000 feet over Roscoe Inlet and was beginning to skim through layers of low stratus and light snow flurries, I tuned the Automatic Direction Finder (ADF) to the Ethelda Bay non-directional beacon and watched the needle swing to that station. By flying straight on the needle I would be able to save 16 minutes flight time. I felt it was worth trying.

I cleared Florence Peninsula at 2500 feet and ran into moderate turbulence and bad visibility. I was about to turn back when I broke into the clear. Off to the southwest I saw the weather improving so I stayed on course, planning to pass Pooley Island, off Don Peninsula, then proceed down Graham Reach which is the main inland waterway leading to Prince Rupert. There was still excessive turbulence and I could see by the water below I would never make it into Klemtu, nor Butedale either. I let Ocean Falls know this and received Red's "Roger, Roger" reply. I crossed Don Peninsula but had to drop to 1500 feet to get under the cloud layer and immediately picked up Pooley Island dead ahead. I noticed the ceiling appeared even lower there . . and that was the instant when I came up to *my* imaginary base line of self-set standard . . . and crossed over.

What follows would never have taken place if I

had had even one passenger. Like a responsible citizen who automatically drives a little slower when he has passengers in his car, my passengers are an inhibiting factor too. Anyway, being alone and anxious to get back to base before dark, I crossed my line.

To stay under the cloud, I decided to fly through the valley that crosses Pooley Island from east to west. The valley, more a canyon, is narrow with rocky bluffs on either side rising sharply to 2500 or 3000 feet. The bottom is a creek bed with some swamp and muskeg clearings. It is about nine miles long and the west end is corked by a saddle requiring 1100 feet altitude to clear.

Half way up the valley I could just see the saddle ahead, though periodically it would be obscured by the cloud I was under. Knowing I would see better lower, I went down to treetop level. That was better. Now I could see the saddle quite clearly. I was a little uneasy now. I was leaving myself only one course and that was straight ahead. At this low level the valley walls were too close together to make a 180-degree turn.

Now the saddle was only two miles ahead. I was hugging the rock on my left as close as I dared without scraping the wing off and keeping my eyes glued on that damn saddle which would disappear and reappear in the cloud. Every instinct was telling me to reverse my heading but a quick look at the other side of the valley, no more than 500 feet away, made my back hair stand on end. I was now committed. I had no room to turn. My hands were sweating and I was sitting erect. Then the saddle vanished completely.

I had only one choice. To go back was impossible and a climb straight ahead was impossible. Micro seconds counted. I knew I needed speed and altitude and I would need that special grace of a pilot's religion if I was to survive the next seconds.

I pushed the nose down slightly and hit the throttles and prop controls at the same time. Almost in despair, I watched the airspeed climb agonizingly toward 165 miles an hour. I was just above the scrubby spruce trees.

I have to explain that the carburetor of a Grumman Goose flying boat works on a float system, like an automobile. Fuel will not flow through it and then to the engine if it is upside down. A Goose is not designed for aerobatics.

The manoeuver I was being forced into was my only hope but it was dead against my instincts vainly warning "no". At treetop level, engines screaming, airspeed over 165, I pulled the stick back sharply and to the right. A split second later I was encased in cloud and upside down, on a reverse heading.

Both engines began to cough, cutout, catch, cough, cutout, catch, right on cue. I knew the instruments were going crazy but there was no time to check. The crate was shuddering in frenzied protest, indicating "stall". My eyes were glued to the artificial horizon instrument, the needle and ball and the rapidly dropping airspeed. Then, out of madness I guess for it wasn't instinct, because I was out of my VFR element, I apparently semi-righted the ship because the engines came back to life, propellors out of synchronization.

My only way was down and out of the cloud and although dizzy with vertigo, I pushed the stick forward. The Goose shook all over but in an instant was in the clear, in too steep a dive with insufficient airspeed. The engines were in unison again but they were protesting at the torture treatment. Easing back, I righted the ship while watching the airspeed pick up slowly. I was headed into a small slough, careening between the surrounding spears of dead spruce. I levelled off just above the ground and watched the airspeed build and at the last possible second, just as I was about to plunge into the trees at the end of the slough, I pulled back on the column and waited. I could do nothing more. She would or she wouldn't.

She did. She climbed out just over the trees with only inches to spare. The capabilities of a Goose aircraft always astound me.

Dead ahead was Mathieson Channel and a minute later I was back over it, on course Prince Rupert. I was cold, clammy, my shirt soaked with sweat. The episode had taken less than two minutes.

During the next hour, I settled back and thought it out. I decided that in those few seconds I had earned all the flying pay of my career. The second thing I decided was that I had crossed my imaginary line of survival. Most important, I resolved I would never cross it again and I never did.

Arrival time at Prince Rupert was 16:28 hours.

Zero - Zero - Seven
versus Zero - Seven - Zero

I HAD MADE all the entries in the company's log book and was starting to complete my own log. The date was December 31, last day of the year. I should phone home, I thought, and check if Anna needs any last minute thing for the New Year's party.

George, my engineer-dispatcher, stuck his head around the door just then. "Anything on HGX, captain?" he asked. I noticed the time was 15:40, making HGX 20 minutes overdue from Sandspit on the Queen Charlottes. "Not a thing," I said, "Give him another call." He went to the transmitter, noted the time in the radio log and called: "HGX, Prince Rupert, do you read? HGX, Rupert, HGX, Rupert, do you read?" Except for atmospheric crackle there was silence.

"Try Sandspit, George. See if they have heard from him." George switched channels and called Sandspit to receive the reply: "Negative on HGX since he switched to radio range at 14:30." George went back: "HGX is 20 minutes overdue. Will give him 10 more minutes before contacting Vancouver." Sandspit signed off with: "Check okay. We are right down in heavy snow now." George leaned back and said: "What do you think, Justin?"

"Dammit, I wish I knew. He should be here by now. I came out of the snow half way across the Strait. He came off Sandspit 10 minutes behind me and I heard him switching to radio range. That was the last time I heard him. Let's sit tight for another 20 minutes."

George went off to the hangar saying he was making up an order for some spares. "Do you need anything," he asked. I told him to request a couple of pilots so I could get some time off. He laughed as he closed the door.

Putting the logs away I tidied up, then realizing Beaver CF-HGX was now 32 minutes overdue, I called him four times on different radio channels. There was no answer so I phoned the Department of Transport radio station on Digby Island and asked the operator to try Joe on his LF and VHF. Still no reply, I called Sandspit again to advise of the circumstances, then switching channels, called the Vancouver head office. Now HGX was 45 minutes overdue. Vancouver took the information and with the main base's powerful transmitter advised all Pacific coast stations to listen for any messages from HGX. The office also advised Air-Sea Rescue in Vancouver and when that happened a complex, well-trained organization went into action.

There are four Rescue Coordination Centres across Canada which we call the RCC. The Pacific centre's area comprises all British Columbia, part of the Northwest Territories, all of the Yukon and the coastal water out 700 miles. It was formed in 1947 under the RCAF and it has at its disposal vast air, ground and marine facilities. The air and marine aspects are split into primary and secondary units.

Primary air facilities include five Albatross flying boats and two Labrador helicopters, all stationed at Comox, Vancouver Island. There is also the Secondary air facilities with three DC3's, one T33 jet and two Neptunes together with three RCMP aircraft. There is one Canadian Coast Guard helicopter on board the cutter *Canso*.

Primary marine facilities are the two 18-knot, 95-ft. Coast Guard cutters, *Ready* and *Racer*, two 45-foot crashboats, *Mallard* and *Moorhen*, the *Canso* and a large hovercraft. Secondary marine facilities calls in when needed the four vessels of the Department of Energy, Mines and Resources, the four vessels of the Department of Public Works, the seven boats of the Department of Fisheries and the twelve coast patrol boats of the RCMP.

Various army units are used for the search on the ground. Normal flight crew aboard most of the aircraft during a search is usually eight or nine people, including spotters.

RCC categorizes a call for assistance into one of three phases: "Uncertainty", "Alert" and "Distress". Uncertainty Phase is when the pilot has not filed an arrival report within 30 minutes of his given estimated time of arrival (called ETA) at an airport served by Air Traffic Control (called ATC)—or 60 minutes after his ETA at an airport not served by ATC—or 24 hours after the time indicated on a filed flight notification. During this phase the DOT and the RCC attempt to locate the missing aircraft by communicating with all known landing areas along the planned flight route.

The Alert Phase comes when the RCC check fails to find the overdue aircraft or if an aircraft cleared to land, fails to land within five minutes, or information comes that the operating efficiency of an aircraft has placed it in danger. During this phase, RCC alerts a rescue unit to prepare aircraft and personnel and it starts plans for the initial search.

The Distress Phase goes into operation when time has run out for the fuel on board the missing aircraft and it is apparent the craft will not make it to safety, or when an aircraft has or is about to make a forced landing. In this phase, RCC is coordinating the search and dispatches all facilities to begin the search.

Primary and Secondary aircraft facilities are on 30-minute standby. Primary and Secondary units of the Marine facility are on immediate standby.

Primary search for a missing aircraft is confined to an area along the planned flight of the aircraft and this area extends for 20 miles on either side of the filed flight path. Pilots are cautioned that if they divert more than 20 miles either side of their route, chances of location and rescue are reduced.

RCC, Vancouver, has direct line communication with all the other facilities, Canada-wide, and has at its disposal, aircraft as far east as Winnipeg and north to the Yukon. In addition, there is a direct line to the U.S. Coast Guard Service in Seattle which directs the Air-Sea Rescue Service in Alaska's southern panhandle. The two teams work together closely.

The entire Air-Sea Rescue system in Canada now operates under the direction of the Canadian Armed Forces. All services, be they for a person or corporation, are made at no cost.

RCC, Pacific Area, in 1966 was concerned with 961 incidents, almost three a day, and directed over 750 hours of flight search. In 1967, there were 966 incidents and 1,258 hours were flown by dedicated men during searches. One search in February, 1968, for three men in a new, twin-engined, Cessna 320 Skynight, involved hundreds of men, took 30 days, totalled 635 flight hours and combed and recombed an area of 84,275 square miles which is a third larger than all the Maritime provinces combined. It was a failure. This was the machine put into motion by my communication to the Vancouver dispatcher and by his call to the Rescue Coordinating Centre.

. . . But all I could do for the moment was sit and sweat. The weather was poor with a forecast of snow and overnight gale force winds of 45 miles an hour. It was no night to be stranded on a lonely beach in a small aircraft, especially New Year's Eve.

Just then, the large turbojet helicopter of the DOT's Prince Rupert Air-Sea Rescue division, dropped to its base next our hangar and when it had been rolled in, I phoned. "Dutch" said on the way up from Vancouver he'd had a hell of a time from Bella Bella north. Coming up the Inside Passage, he'd been forced to land on the water several times because of poor visibility in moderate to heavy snow. He said he hadn't come out of the snow until he was 10 miles south of Prince Rupert. When I told him of our situation he replied he would undoubtedly be getting word from Vancouver momentarily.

It was 16:20, 15 minutes before grounding time, and the first few flakes were beginning to melt on the window. George came in with a couple of Pacific Western Airline pilots just as Vancouver called on the long distance phone. I was told that HGX had been heard from. He was on the water in Principe Channel holding due to heavy snow. His radio call was answered but there was no acknowledgement. I told Vancouver his reported position puzzled me since it was 90 miles off course to the southeast of Prince Rupert. I added the weather system moving in made it impossible to begin an immediate search and I could only hope he had been able to find a sheltered bay where he could beach the aircraft for the night. I said if he did not arrive by daybreak next morning, I would begin a search.

Our company's business is seasonal. Summer is extremely busy and the winter is slack. Pilots take their vacations between October and March and senior pilots have first choice of the period they want off. This arrangement allows the company to retain all its trained pilots by using them for relief duty at the remote bases. The most experienced junior pilots usually relieve at a base where a single pilot is based, like myself. Each summer the company hires five or six new pilots to meet the needs of the continually expanding service and they spend the summer gaining experience with the machines and policies, acquiring a precise knowledge of the coastline. The training programs work from the main base at Vancouver and the two major bases of Campbell River and Port Hardy. By October, the new pilots are qualified and capable of assuming a relief pilot's responsibility at a remote base, while the pilot-in-charge is getting a tan and rejuvenating his bones in Hawaii, where a lot of us go.

The company has a problem finding new pilots who have special aptitudes for meeting the unusual conditions prevalent at such bases as Ocean Falls,

Sandspit and Prince Rupert and they must adapt to the firm's rigid safety standards. The winter weather at Sandspit and Prince Rupert can be hairy and because of this, emphasis is placed on flying the radio range legs and adhering to a given course with the use of directional gyros and automatic direction finders. It is not possible to emphasize fully the importance of such knowledge specially for the flight across Hecate Strait between Prince Rupert and Sandspit. That 100 miles is infamous for some of the world's worst flying weather.

Joe, out there somewhere on this dirty New Year's Eve, for a time had flown out of Prince Rupert and he had been based at Port Hardy a year. Previous to his latest arrival in Rupert, where his wife lived, he had spent a month at Ocean Falls. On December 23, I had taken him over to Sandspit on my scheduled flight, where he would base for a 10-day relief period, while the regular pilot took time off. Unusually heavy snow had closed most of the Queen Charlotte logging and mining operations and it became a quiet period for him. Basically he was on standby, for emergencies only.

Today, December 31, I had flown the Goose from Rupert to Sandspit on my regular scheduled run, but instead of continuing south, the weather forced me to hold at Sandspit for two hours. With no sign of letup, at the end of that time I scrubbed the rest of the flight and returned to Rupert. Joe was itching to get to Rupert to spend New Year's with his wife and knowing from old we seldom were called out on New Year's Day, I agreed he could fly his Beaver over and that he would return to Sandspit on the 2nd unless needed sooner. I was airborne at 14:10 with five passengers and I heard Joe in HGX take off behind me at 14:21. Now it was 17:30.

There was another call from Vancouver. The

operations manager asked me if I had seen Joe's wife. I said I would leave a watch on the radio and go at once. Bonnie opened the door.

"Come on in Justin. Where's Joe?"

"I came by to tell you he had a problem after reaching the mainland from Sandspit and I'm afraid he's going to have to spend the night on the beach."

I said he'd probably be in by daylight next morning and not to worry. She said she would spend the evening with friends. As I drove home in the blizzard, I was hoping he really had been able to beach because the heavy wet snow would soon sink the Beaver from sheer weight. Anna was all fixed up for the party we were supposed to attend but as an understanding airman's wife, she adapted to staying home so I could be near the phone and the shortwave radio. Midnight came, me poring over the area charts and Anna pouring coffee. The wind was steady at 50 miles an hour and the snow was building. By 3 a.m., I just had to get some sleep for what I knew was ahead, and went to bed.

When I wakened three hours later, the snow had stopped, the wind had died, there were cloud patches and it seemed we would even have some sun. The crew was waiting for me at the hangar at 07:00 and we were airborne for Principe Channel at 07:45. We were confident we would find the Beaver in a few minutes and I had enough men on board to get her back into the water and homeward bound.

South from Rupert, I cut southeast of Porcher Island, through Ogden Channel and took the east side of Macauly Island thinking Joe might have sought shelter in Petrel Channel. I came out into Principe Channel and skimmed along the east side checking all the logical places that might provide a night's mooring.

Minktrap Bay would be a good spot I thought, but there was nothing there but desolation. I went down the west side of Principe. Nothing there either. I went round Macauly Island again and peered into every cranny that could possibly hold an aircraft, around the outlying rock specks, went into Principe again looking deeper into the fingers. Nothing. My search area that morning varied from 40 to 100 miles south of Prince Rupert but something didn't ring true and I couldn't put my finger on it. Joe knew the area and I had to assume he had given a correct position report but Principe Channel was just too far off his course. It was a puzzle. I radioed Rupert and said I would try still further south and then east should he have tried to get into Grenville Channel.

About then I was joined by a Beaver that Pacific Western Airlines had sent with two pilots and it was able to get further into the tight inlets than I had been able to with my fatter Grumman Goose. By noon, running short of fuel, I headed back to Rupert.

Calling Vancouver, I was told that two Beavers were en route from the south and the RCC had dispatched two RCAF Albatrosses. Joe was now 18 hours overdue.

Taking two more spotters aboard for a crew of seven, I headed out of Rupert again, south down Grenville Channel checking every inlet, bay and beach. I flew the entire length with no luck. Then I started zipping about some of the islands at the mouth of Douglas Channel, 95 miles south of Rupert, and I landed at Ethelda Bay to check the DOT station there. The staff had not seen or heard anything the night before.

The weather was starting to return. By 14:40, snow squalls were showing up and visibility was decreasing to the point we knew we were missing areas. By now, the search had been joined by our two Beavers from the south, the DOT helicopter from Prince Rupert, the two big Albatrosses from Vancouver and two more Beavers from Pacific Western. Traffic was beginning to be a problem specially with the decreasing visibility. We were in continual contact with each other and the Albatrosses, equipped with radar, were able to keep out of the way but it became so confusing we all returned to Rupert to set up a headquarters and a search pattern under Capt. Ormsby of the DOT.

At 15:30, I took off for one more hour's patrol thinking to cover Porcher Island and the little islands in its vicinity. There was only an hour's flight time left before dark and in light to moderate snow my spotters and I covered every possible spot he could have set down in or taxied to. I returned to Rupert, depressed and dog-tired. I had flown seven hours on three hours sleep.

Everybody met at the search headquarters that night and we decided on a checker pattern search plan to keep us apart for safety, and ensure we would not miss a section. I went home to bed at 21:00, to find Anna had kept some of the kids' New Year's turkey hot, but I had no appetite. It was hellish weather for a man to be stranded.

Next morning, January 2, at 07:45, my spotters and I took off for our area, Macauly Island. We flew a criss-cross east and west pattern, then a criss-cross north and south pattern, then a criss-cross diagonal pattern and it took us well over an hour with no sign of the other searchers. The other eight aircraft meanwhile were flying areas both north and south of Rupert. I asked permission by radio to go further south than yesterday and that given I went down Principe, passed Trutch Island and Compania Island, into Laredo Channel, checking all the inlets on the west side of Princess Royal Island. It was a tough job as the inlets are long and the snow made visibility bad. By noon I was on the Rupert ramp more depressed than ever.

I was told the DOT's marine division now had a vessel checking out the entrance to Principe Channel and was using lifeboats to check the shorelines for debris. After a sandwich and some fuel we headed off again to another search area. Visibility was a little better and heading down Petrel Channel into Principe, by God, there was a big oil slick. I circled it low for 10 minutes and then landed, but once I was on the water couldn't find it again. On my radio report, Rupert dispatched one of the Albatrosses but before it could find us marking the spot for it, I was forced to head for Rupert to get back before dark.

Another headquarters meeting was held that night and it was interesting to get the comments from the other pilots and hear what had been told them when they had made landings. Wally Russell, our operations manager up from the south for the search, said he landed at Kitkatlah Indian village and the chief said he had seen the aircraft overhead but he put the time as 13:00 and HGX was still at Sandspit then. A radio report came in from the DOT ship, anchored for the night at Port Stephens in Principe Channel, and the captain said he had interviewed two fishermen whose statements were identical. On New Year's Eve, they had seen a Beaver with our markings going up the channel, low in heavy snow and they had been surprised to see one out in such weather. A few minutes later they heard but didn't see what sounded to be the same machine going past them in the opposite direction. Then, 15 minutes later, they heard the distinctive thrumming whirr and high-pitched turbo whine they recognized as the DOT helicopter. Their times agreed with the helicopter's arrival time in Prince Rupert and the time HGX should have been in Principe Channel.

We decided the search craft would concentrate on an area further south next day but I would go back to the area of the oil slick and meet the DOT ship which would pick up an oil sample to be sent to Vancouver for analysis. It would be easy to find out if the oil did indeed come from one of our airplanes. By now we were so tired we could hardly think straight and it took any remaining energy we had to undergo the questions of newsmen for by now the story was getting a lot of attention.

Next morning it was 10:00 hours before we were airborne, owing to the snow. This time I found the oil slick first try and could see the DOT vessel five miles away down channel. I went down, circled it, then went back over the oil and kept circling there to mark the captain's way. I landed on the water and waited for him and when he came he put over a lifeboat, bottled a sample of oil off the surface and passed it to one of my crew. I took off at once for Digby Island airport where a fighter jet from Comox was waiting. It had flown the length of the coast in under an hour and in less than two hours after it left on the return leg we would have the analysis report.

I was on the tarmac discussing the search with a group when one of the DOT radio operators came out of the terminal building on the run, calling: "HGX has been located! We've just had the word!"

All he knew was the Trans-Provincial Airline at

Terrace had reported a charter of theirs had flown down Douglas Channel for Swindle Island further down the mainland and it had gone directly over a small point south of Gill Island. There in Barnard Harbour the pilot had spotted the Beaver. He had landed, picked up Joe and had returned to Terrace.

It was decided one of the Albatrosses would leave at once for Terrace and bring Joe to Rupert, then one by one each of the search planes were contacted and directed to return to base. To say we were happy would be an understatement.

The Albatross waddled up the Seal Cove amphibian ramp just before dark and the hundred-odd pilots, crews and ground crews who had been working their heads off gathered round the door to lend a hero's welcome. Joe was barely recognizable, unshaven of course, white, weak and obviously suffering from shock and exposure. There was no point starting the questions and he was speeded to the Prince Rupert General hospital. So many searches up and down the B.C. coast end in failure, it was with the feeling concerted teamwork had beaten the odds we all retired to headquarters and more than one bottle was opened that night. It was quite a party.

At the same time, there was an undercurrent that something was not right. Not one of the aircraft had spotted him although each at one time had been within yards of him. I could count at least three times I had been over Barnard Harbour myself.

Next morning, all the searchers headed out of Rupert for their bases with our utmost thanks and that afternoon Russell and I interviewed Joe to get his statement.

When he took off from Sandspit, he said, he had

an idea his compass had gone dead but he had continued on the same radio range heading knowing that clear weather was ahead. At the mainland he found himself in heavy snow and entered a narrow inlet he realized later to be Otter Passage just north of Ethelda Bay. Then he began going up Principe Channel. He landed because of the poor visibility, turned around, took off again and headed down channel hoping to get into Grenville Channel and out of the snow. Again he was forced to land he said, and this time he radioed his position and the reason he was on the water. He said he had called several times but heard no acknowledgements. Then, in a lull he took off a third time, went up Otter Channel, went into heavy snow again and was forced down on the south end of Gill Island where he had taxied up on the beach in a small cove. At that point, Joe said, he had no idea where he was. He added that the Beaver, HGX, had taken some jolting in his last landing.

On the beach for three days, Joe said he kept large fires going all the time and had tried to make a lot of smoke. He stated firmly that not once had he heard an aircraft overhead.

In the meantime, the company sent a pilot and a couple of engineers to Barnard Harbour to check out HGX. They returned to Rupert reporting the Beaver had taken a lot of damage to the floats, spreader bars and undercarriage but with spares it could be repaired on the beach and then flown to Vancouver for a complete check.

The most intriguing report came from the pilot, who after throwing the master switch, had flicked on the radio and instantly had been in contact with the company transmitters at Port Hardy, Campbell River,

Prince Rupert, Sandspit and Vancouver. The radio was a little out of tune but otherwise perfect. It was stated also there were no signs of beach fires; there was extensive driftwood in all directions; close by there was a big spruce with a large split oozing quantities of pitch that would have made a good beacon fire; the compass was in perfect working order and so was the directional gyro. More mystery. Joe was put on the suspension list and the company's investigation moved to the Vancouver head office.

To summarize that enquiry, it was soon apparent Joe had found some kind of unexplained difficulty tuning to the radio range frequency. He had therefore flown through the range leg and had taken up a heading he felt was the heading of the radio range.

This heading should have been *zero zero seven degrees*.

Instead he had taken the heading of *zero seven zero degrees*.

There was little wind but the little there was would have drifted him north of the range leg, not south. Where he came upon the mainland was in fact the point he would have reached had he held a 070 degree heading all the way from Sandspit.

It was further decided the radio calls he made to Vancouver were actually made from Barnard Harbour and beyond any doubt had made them while the Beaver was on the beach after it had sustained the damage.

Joe was fired.

It is hard to estimate the costs involved in an aircraft search. There is flying time, operating costs, loss of revenue for the aircraft joining the search and the cost to the taxpayer for the RCAF participation.

Our own company costs totalled about $3500, apart from staff time. If the search is a failure, as it often is, time usually turns up the answer. Years may go by but a file is never closed until time and a wandering trapper happens upon the scarred and sometimes skeletal remains.

I spoke with Joe many times following his dismissal and to give him credit, he stuck steadfastly to his story that he had been on a 007 heading in spite of all contrary evidence he had flown a 070. It was a point to be argued for months but the evidence was clear to all. There was no doubt it had been . . "finger trouble".

He is now a first officer flying a large corporation aircraft in eastern Canada—and his name isn't Joe. I hear he is doing well and I wish him luck. Perhaps he has learned the one all-important airman's commandment: thou shall be alert at all times.

There is a footnote. The oil slick I found in Principe Channel, through the analysis, turned out to be seepage from a massive petroleum deposit in a subterranean channel and oil companies are now conducting extensive underwater tests. I should have staked a claim.

Charters are Fun
...Sometimes

CHARTERS ACCOUNT for a fair percentage of a light aircraft company's business. A charter is a flight that is apart from the regular schedule and is usually to a destination that is not a customary port of call, hired by a person or company like a taxicab in town. No special aircraft are reserved for charter work, nor are there special pilots. The aircraft used depends on the nature of the charter, the number of passengers, the amount and type of freight, the distance to be flown and the kind of landing to be made. Regular airplanes are used and like the pilots, schedules have to be shuffled to fit them in. Sometimes I think it is no wonder operations managers are tough to live with.

Few charters are routine, from point A to point B. Weather is of course the most important indeterminate. Then there is the water condition, the size of the lake the charterer wants to land in, how protected it is by high mountains and the kind and quantity of freight.

The aspect most un-routine is the charterer him-self. There is the single prospector who wants to be taken into a part of the B.C. hinterland I swear only God knows about, with three months food supply, tent, hardware and all his other equipment, and God willing, you have to pick him up three months later at the same place. There are the well-to-do types, sometimes couples, who take a Beaver for two or three weeks and fish the most remote lakes the pilot can find. I often wonder if they ever calculate the cost of getting the fish against the per pound weight of the fish they catch.

There are the strictly-business charters for fisheries inspectors to count the fish boats in a given area in a certain season; forestry men to plot the outline of a forest fire or to take a look at an incipient fire reported by a fire watchtower lookout; industrial photographers with assignments to get certain aerial views; mining equipment engineers making a round-robin circuit of locations where their machinery is installed.

Then there is the damn freight—45-gallon drums of fuel, engine blocks for big Cat's, great pieces of un-relenting machinery for the mines and camps, mountains of groceries, sacks of mail specially at Christmas—name it and I have humped every item imaginable thought necessary for life or industry. A bush pilot is no air jockey. He doesn't just sit there and fly the plane. On charter trips specially, he is also his own freight handler—getting it aboard, tieing it down, manhandling it to the dock when he gets there—and most times he climbs wearily back into the cockpit to fly home, almost too pooped to participate.

On a charter there is the opportunity to know people that is not possible in the day-to-day scheduled operation. The charterer usually sits in the co-pilot's seat beside you and a certain camaraderie develops that often makes for a lasting friendship. A few times I've even had to share the same sleeping bag with my charter and if you don't think that doesn't make an impression, try it. Most are knowledgeable, understanding, sympathetic and appreciative, but every so often there is the clot who demands to press on even though the weather is zero zero. How many times have I heard a passenger say to an agent, after being told his scheduled flight had been cancelled due to weather: "in that case I'll charter"!

I remember an incident when a particularly arrogant president of a major coast company, with two of his executives, arrived at Port Hardy by scheduled airliner. He had flown with us hundreds of times and his reputation among us for his treatment of pilots was not nice. The weather was terrible, so bad in fact, we had scrubbed the rest of the day's operations because of snow and freezing rain. Our agent half fearfully, told him his reserved charter had been cancelled for the day. He was livid. He would have that charter or else, he said. I was Joe that day and I tried all my few charms, then arguments, then haggling, then I thought, if you want it so badly, I'll *show* you and I'll scare you so you'll finally learn a lesson. The three of them sloshed across the tarmac into the Beaver and with a brief warmup I headed across Johnstone Strait toward Cape Caution, their destination.

Twenty minutes from takeoff, I could see them start looking uneasily at each other. I knew I wasn't going to finish the flight but they would have to tell me to turn around. Don't misunderstand. If it is an emergency we will fly in any kind of weather barring fog or zero visibility. We were quite safe but only I knew that. There was some ice on the wings and the rain and snow made visibility poor but not impossible.

We were 200 feet above the tossing gray sea. I was really enjoying it for the first time in a long time. The window iced over on the co-pilot's side where he was sitting but I had a vent on my side giving me a patch of clear view. He clutched my arm and his pleading look told me he'd had enough. I reversed heading and went back to Hardy. I saw them an hour later in the airport coffee shop. Their hands were still shaking and I heard he never bullied a pilot again.

Most charters were fun and the best were those with an element of surprise. The Department of Fisheries was building a fish ladder in a stream and the crew asked to be chartered out of Port Hardy to a tiny lake and picked up weeks later. There was a ton of equipment and supplies and we loaded two Beavers and took off, one behind the other. When I came over the speck as lead plane, I circled it a half dozen times trying to figure out how I could get off once I had got on. I radioed the other aircraft to circle and watch me. It was a tight landing on a mere puddle surrounded by tall trees. As I turned around at the end of my taxi run, there was Dave coming in. He said later he hadn't heard my message. Dave was unloaded first so he taxied around a bit to rough up the water (takeoff on smooth water takes a greater distance) then attempted to lift off but he had to abort at the last minute. I decided to try from the opposite end so I taxied down, turned around and let the breeze drift me back into the weeds, gunned her with all she had, held on the step until the airspeed built, lifted off, then kept the nose close to the water and at the last second pulled back and cleared the trees with feet to spare. I circled and told the other pilot to do the same thing and we returned to base together. Freighting went on continually for three months and every liftoff was exciting. Some of the boys at Hardy refused to go near the place and I couldn't blame them.

Then there were the two prospectors who wanted off at a remote and particularly desolate bit of beach on the west coast of the Queen Charlottes. I was packed high with their groceries and supplies and an aluminum boat was strapped outside. I was able to land the Beaver on the crest of the three-foot chop but the water was too rough to let the waves deposit me on the beach and I had to hold her off with the engine while the partners got soaked on the float releasing the boat. It flipped sideways into the water and swamped. It slid under a pontoon and I thought I was going to be holed for sure. They jumped into the chest-high water with waves breaking over their heads, managed to pull the boat out and then let it drift to the beach. One box at a time, they carried each of their boxes on their heads to shore. It took them 45 minutes and all that time I jockeyed the waves to keep from being shipwrecked.

A wry sense of humour caused another near shipwreck. The perpetrator was Alan Best, curator of Vancouver's Stanley Park zoo, brother of Gordon Best, the company's former chief executive. On Princess Royal Island, half way between Ocean Falls and Prince Rupert, lives the unique Kermode bear. He is like a black bear except for his cinnamony-white colour. Alan got word one was making a nuisance of himself around an Indian village and thinking he would made a distinctive specimen for the zoo, chartered a Cessna 180 to go get him. Nobby Haider who was handed the assignment, had just started with the company the day before, didn't know the coast well and understandably was nervous going so far out of Vancouver in a 180. He and Alan made the island on the nose, found the bear, subdued him with a hypodermic dart, wrapped him in a bundle of wire fencing and started home, their knocked-out passenger on the floor behind. Nobby was carefully watching his compass and chart, proudly picking up the landmarks one by one, heading for Ocean Falls to refuel before continuing into Vancouver, when the anaesthetic effect began subsiding. The bear became restless and began to growl. Nobby knew damn well the bear was secure in his steel bag but a growling bear eighteen inches from his rear end, was not an ideal situation and he was getting nervous. He inched forward in the seat, kept staring ahead, concentrating on the growling coastline below while the ominous growls grew louder behind. Alan was watching with a sardonic grin and schoolboyishly, he quietly moved his left arm up and behind Nobby's shoulder. Next time the bear growled, his big hand clamped down tight. The pilot's reaction was instantaneous. Whap! The little ship went straight up, then straight down. It was 15 minutes before Nobby could scrape himself off the ceiling and fly a straight route again. You can still visit that bear in Stanley Park. While there, judge for yourself if Alan Best's sense of fun now seems more subdued.

The charter that was the most fun was my longest—10 days and 4,000 miles. Except for about 15 miles, it was all within British Columbia. There was seven months preparation.

I first met Herb McDonald in the summer of '64 when he tape recorded an interview with me in Prince Rupert. I was one of some 350 interviewees he talked to all over the province for a book on B.C. life he was researching. The next day, he was a passenger on my scheduled run to the Queen Charlottes where I dropped him at the large MacMillan Bloedel, Juskatla logging camp. I was to pick him up two days later to return him to Rupert, but the weather that day was in the form of a specially nasty fog that shrouds the Charlottes at times. That day, I left Sandspit heading north for Masset, then to Rupert, knowing darn well I wouldn't be able to get into Juskatla. I flew low up the Charlotte coast under the fog, following the shore at low level. I received a weather report from the Juskatla agent who said there was three miles visibility there, so I acknowledged and said I would be in for McDonald. I went around the north end of the island, passed over Masset, then headed south down the Masset canal, watching for the break that was supposed to be around Juskatla. When I came over the camp visibility was almost zero, but with some luck I found a thinner spot and was able to land on the water. McDonald, the agent, and others were on the ramp and they were surprised I had come in. I told them they were all damn poor judges of visibility distance but the agent said what I thought was miles, was instead, feet. I had misunderstood him. It was a hairy takeoff through the Juskatla goo, but clear at Masset for a landing and the trip across the Strait was lovely. When McDonald left Rupert, heading south on CPA, I thought I would never see him again due to that Juskatla ball-up.

He called me from Vancouver the following December. He had been assigned by the British Columbia Centennial Committee to produce a book, half pictures, half text, to depict the province as it ended its first century. It would be published in the fall of 1966,

Herbert L. McDonald

Justin de Goutiere, 1926 - 1968

*The last portrait made of the author during the period
he was stationed at Prince Rupert*

THESE PHOTOGRAPHS will provide the reader some visualization of the types of small aircraft mentioned in the text which are providing the principal communication along the Pacific coast of British Columbia in the late 1960's, together with an indication of the settings described by the author. The uncredited photos were taken by him, here reproduced from his original colour transparencies.

GRUMMAN MALLARD, CF-HPU, cruises at 165 mph, carrying 11 passengers and a crew of two, over a coast inlet en route to Ocean Falls. This type was built in the late 1940's as an executive amphibian. Only 54 were produced. Three still operate on the B.C. coast, all owned by B.C. Air Lines Ltd. Don Leblanc photo.

THIS SCENE could have been photographed in any
one of thousands of hidden lakes tucked among
the high mountains as here a moored Goose awaits
the return of its charter fishing party.

GRUMMAN GOOSE, CF-RQI, *trundles out of the
sea up a coastal ramp. First built in wartime for coast patrol, there are now only ten
in B.C. — six commercial, four corporate.*

JOHN BOAK, 45, killed while landing at Vancouver airport, 1968, well known on the coast, had a distinguished record during war with Royal Navy's Fleet Air Arm.

B.C. AIR LINES was Canada's first commercial air carrier to transport a reigning British monarch. Two Mallards flew Queen Elizabeth's party on a fishing trip, 1959.

TINY TIDAL BAY *becomes a snug, up-coast harbour for a Beaver, chartered by a timber cruiser who is ashore checking amount and type of the area's timber.*

STUCK IN THE MUD *from a receding tide, this is Goose aircraft and scene described in Chapter Four. Almost all B.C. coast pilots have experienced this at least once.*

Northwest of Kemano, site of the Alcan Company's Kitimat power house, the aut

man Goose is en route from Bella Coola to Prince Rupert, on course at 10,000 feet.

BEAVER, CF-HGZ, moored to a bank on the Omineca River, in front of the Westfall's Germansen Landing trading post described in Chapter Seven.

ROSE SPIT, the northern tip of the Queen Charlotte Islands, is a wind and wave formed needle of sand that arcs gracefully into Dixon Entrance.

MOUNT ROBSON, 12,972 feet of icy majesty, photographed from Beaver, CF-HGZ, during the 4,000 mile charter flight described in Chapter Seven.

LIKE BALLS OF COTTON, fleecy white cumulus clouds float in front of the author's Beaver at 12,500 feet.

MIDSUMMER comes to the mountains near Kemano. These are in the same general area as those in the larger photo, overleaf, taken in early spring.

KLEMTU on Finlayson Channel is a tiny fishing community on the Inner Passage used by all the cruise ships between Vancouver and Alaska.

NEW DE HAVILLAND TWIN OTTER, as described in the Epilogue, can land in 500 feet with 18 passengers. Here pictured by Don Leblanc at Vancouver's International airport, it represents an investment of over $550,000 — a far cry from B.C. Air Lines' first two-place Luscombe, costing $4,000.

WASHED ASHORE on the Sechelt Peninsula, this is the wreck of the Sea Bee aircraft that is featured in the Bill Waddington
1949 story narrated in Chapter Ten.

NORSEMAN AIRCRAFT has become an
aerial ambulance as it arrives at Campbell
River with an injured man. See Chapter Eight.
This is a Campbell River Courier photo.

A BOEING-VERTOL HELICOPTER, known in the Canadian Armed Forces as the CH-113 Labrador, is the 25-passenger capacity machine used by the Search and Rescue Unit. (Chapter Six.) Two are stationed at the Comox base, Vancouver Island, and have been occupied in aerial searches almost daily since their acquisition. (CAF Photo.)

TWENTY YEARS SEPARATE these two Canadian Pacific Airline photographs. Now known as CP Air, it is one of Vancouver's largest companies with international connections. Above, the Canso that connected Sandspit with Prince Rupert. Below, one of seven 99-passenger Boeing 737's to appear on CP Air's B.C. routes in 1969.

TWO OPERATIONAL ASPECTS of Vancouver's Pacific Western Airlines, Canada's third largest, are this Otter with Yukon-bound freight and this Boeing 707 jet, pictured at London airport. The $5.25 millions 707 carried 14,000 passengers on 102 charter trips in its first year to places like Grand Cayman, Copenhagen, Hawaii and Mexico.

A BEAVER wings over Tahsis Inlet on Vancouver Island's west coast, a symbol of the communication light aircraft are bringing to the coastal life of British Columbia — a scene repeated many times daily on the 525-mile long timbered shore.

B.C.'s centennial year. Based on knowledge gained from his research in '64, he was planning a long road tour by camper truck and wanted to know if the company and I would be interested to fly him on a long charter that would approximate a clock-wise, outer perimeter circle of the entire province. The aircraft would be used for two reasons, 1) to take specified aerial photographs of certain places, 2) as transportation to certain ground locations that were either too remote by road, impossible to get to by road or that wouldn't dovetail into his 6,000-mile camper truck trip. Of course we said yes.

There were several more calls, then an exchange of many letters and sometimes a few visits with him when a ferry job took me into the Vancouver base. I told him he was out of his mind. He had come up with an involved 10-day schedule that looked as if it had been detailed by a travel agent—times of departures, times of arrivals as many as three and four a day, times we were to meet such and such and so and so. It won't wash I told him. What happens to the schedule, I asked, if on the second day, the weather closes in and we are grounded for 10 hours? He said we'd have to take the chance—a lot of places he wanted to cover only received mail once a month and he had to give them a definite time, but with the provision if we didn't arrive at the specified time to expect us 24 hours later. Any period of bad weather, no matter how short, would delay the charter an extra day. I still didn't think it would work, but his production budget was paying for it and it was his problem.

The office and I planned to use a Cessna 180 amphibian but it became apparent that with the long route he wanted to go plus all the camera equipment he needed, plus the emergency kits I must include, plus his wife and their dog, it would have to be a Beaver with long range tanks. The trouble was we didn't have a Beaver with long range tanks. About two months before departure, by good fortune we acquired just such equipment and since this was the chance to show the company colors around the province, the Prince Rupert crew and I spent three weeks rubbing her down with steel wool, lacquering her red and white, lettering her and cresting her tail with our flying thunderbird symbol. Her engine was taken apart and put together again and every part was checked. Her three radio systems were double-checked. She was certainly fit.

Don't look for a hairy episode in the following. It was a smooth charter with two appreciative people. I include it as the medium which provides a way to describe some of this challenging province apart from the coast and that could not be experienced except by small aircraft. It has no ending except the one of a successful job done well but it does provide an opportunity to meet some vital people of the province and perhaps feel the vitality that is British Columbia today.

The McDonalds left Vancouver by camper truck in time to make the Williams Lake rodeo July 1. From there they continued north to Barkerville where they spent some time in the old mining town that is being restored by the provincial government as a tourist attraction. Up further to Prince George, then west on Highway 16 to Kispiox and Kitwancool, the Indian settlements, they researched and photographed before going down to Kitimat to spend time with the Aluminum company people. Right on schedule on July 15, they arrived at our door and spent a couple of days removing the dust before flying with me on the 17th, on my scheduled run to Juskatla where the Ike Barber's, the M&B manager, were going to house them for a couple of days while they got their logging pictures. They left "Bo", their little white poodle, with us, and he and our old dachshund "Suzie" had a fine time seeing how dirty they could get each other.

On their return from Juskatla, we began loading the Beaver on the afternoon of the 21st and when the camper truck had disgorged its equipment I found secure storage for the truck in downtown Prince Rupert. In warm sunshine, on the schedule made months before, we were off the water and airborne at 14:30 of July 22nd. Maybe it's going to work, I thought, but I doubt it.

It would not be remiss if I interrupted the story to voice some appreciation of aerial photography and photographers. I have flown hundreds of them and I am always impressed by the professionalism with which each attacks his assignment. Now, because of magnificent cameras, precision lenses, fidelity color film and craftsmen, no part of the world is any longer strange to another part and its people. Like the astonishing photographs taken in space by astronauts, aerial photographers working from aircraft are doing much the same thing as they focus on a meandering valley, a mountain-top lake, a craggy peak or a city sprawl.

A Beaver aircraft is the ideal vehicle for the work. The windows in the pilot's and co-pilot's doors slide down into the door even when in flight. This permits shooting into the open air. The wing is high and behind both positions, giving the camera a 60-degree free view almost directly ahead and to the side. If the pilot tilts down his side, thus raising the wing tip on the photographer's side, and crabs a bit, the camera is able to take the whole scene from the sky to the ground almost directly beneath, without a protrusion of any part of the aircraft in the lens. It has lots of room at the photographer's feet for ancillary equipment and the three-person bench behind the pilot and co-pilot's seats, gives a single passenger as Mrs. McDonald was, room to organize other equipment and film to pass forward as needed.

Bo stuck his head out the open window above Prince Rupert, had his ears nearly blown off, whuffed once, climbed back to the bench seat and fell asleep as though he'd been flying all his three years. He flew the entire 4,000 miles with us, most of them asleep and never once disgraced himself. Sometimes we were airborne as long as six straight hours, with never a whimper from him. He is either a most unusual dog or he has tremendous storage.

Herb got some aerials of Rupert and it was then I learned how it was to be for the trip. Every time he saw the scene he wanted, I would have to go around again so he could make sure, then go round again for him to take a light meter reading, then go round again for the first take in color, then go round again for a second take in black and white. He used a Hasselblad camera for the complete job, with many lenses and with different film backs. By switching backs he could duplicate the color shot in black and white immediately. Four or five times for each shot, I thought, brother!

Then we headed up the 125-mile long, scenic inlet called the Portland Canal to Stewart, our first stop. The milky green water, sometimes turquoise, sometimes opalescent, is a sight that always pleased me. We landed on the gravel runway and tied down beside an Okanagan helicopter and a mountain of freight destined for airlift to the Granduc mine under-glacier, tunnel-driving project.

In the gold mining days of the 1920's, Stewart was a substantial city of 27,000 people. For the last 30 years, with perhaps 200 people, it was a village that waited for tomorrow. With the discovery and development of vast copper and molybdenum deposits nearby, Stewart's tomorrow is becoming booming today. As we went over the townsite, circling into the runway, we could see dozens of fine homes under construction in planned developments. One development was being built by the Granduc company and the method was ingenious. A three-sided foundation was built then big trailer trucks at tidewater moved a whole house off a barge that had been towed from the Vancouver area where the house was built, up to the site where bull-dozers manoeuvred the house on to the foundation. The open fourth side was the escape hatch. After that, the fourth wall of the foundation was filled in.

Herb had been there in '64 during his previous research and had met Ian McLeod, a quiet, thirtyish bachelor, former miner, who had inherited a quaint white clapboard pile called the Hotel King Edward, built by his father in the 20's. McLeod had persevered, firm in his miner's belief that one day renewed mining activity would pay off and now it was. He had just finished a small wing of well furnished extra rooms, a dining room sparkling with captain's chairs, china and cutlery, a bar decorated with copper things featuring drinks served in copper mugs.

McLeod's sad old truck was outside and he had told Herb to use it. It didn't have a key, he said—jiggle the wire that stuck out of the dashboard. The three of us went for a walk after dinner in the long twilight.

In mid-summer up there, it doesn't get dark until 11 o'clock. As we neared the hotel, Herb said: "Justin, let's go for a drive. How about we steal that old truck over there and take off." "That's an idea," I said, and jumped in. Helen, who hadn't heard McLeod's offer, stood outside astonished. "What do you two think you're doing?" she said. "The idea!" Meantime I was jiggling the wire which started the wreck. "Get out of there," she said. "That's the way it is here," I told her, "everybody uses everybody else's stuff—nobody minds." But we had to get out and shove her in and we drove down the beach road.

If you look at the map and run an eye up the Portland Canal north of Prince Rupert you will find a finger projecting down from the very end of the inlet. The finger is a mountain ridge and the southern end of the border between Canadian and American territory, between British Columbia and the Alaska Panhandle, meets tidewater down the middle of that ridge. You will see that Stewart is on the Canadian side of the ridge and that a speck of a place called Hyder, is on the American side. The road from Stewart skirts around the ridge, goes into Hyder, then follows the ridge up the American side between it and the Salmon river. The road crosses back into Canadian territory about 11 miles from Hyder, and continues north. Thus a border curiosity exists where the only access by road to the Granduc mine development is through American territory. Many have been the government border regulations that don't even get lip service. As you tootle down the dirt road and cross the border into Hyder, there is an arched sign reading, if it hasn't fallen down since, "The Friendliest Ghost Town in America" and there is no better description. The customs house is a grocery store run by a little old lady who waves vaguely at you as you drive by if she isn't waiting on a customer. At store closing time and Sundays, she closes the shop and leaves the border to its own devices. There are a couple of bars and one, going back to the 20's, is filled with the bric-a-brac of the era. American liquor and cigarettes are sold at American prices, Sundays too, and Stewart people take advantage of the freedom. The Mounties in Stewart try to keep things in moderation and as long as the "smuggling" is kept to a circumspect level without open blandishment, affairs are conducted with intelligent understanding. After a drink in Hyder, we went back to the old King Edward and to bed.

Typical of B.C. northern hospitality, McLeod next morning piloted the three of us, and Bo, around through Hyder in his old truck, and up the Granduc road which at that time was being re-built for heavy mining truck traffic and was in a terrible state. High up on the ridge, 1,000 feet above the valley floor, we crossed back into Canada at a spot marked only by a concrete post. Ian stopped to tell us the story of Dago Marie who built an eight-girl house a few feet inside the American boundary marker in the 20's heyday of gold mining up that valley. Her liquor and women took a lot of the miners' payroll until she was burned out about '26. I understand she's in Portland now, still living off the proceeds.

A mile or so further we came to what on first impression appeared to be a Tibetan lamasery sprawling down the mountainside. It was the abandoned dormitory of the once-famous, now abandoned Silbak Premier gold mine, in the 20's the richest on the continent. Its ore was shipped all the way back to the Stewart dock by overhead buckets on a continuous tram line. Herb had scheduled the stop at Stewart for just one picture. Ian had brought him here in '64 but too late in the day to do natural light photography. Herb had not forgotten the shot and had planned it into the historical chapter of the coming book. Ian had not been back since and didn't know if the shot was still there. Based on chance, we had come a long way to find out.

About 1924, Premier was a booming operation employing at least 2,000 men. High in the aerie retreat 3,000 feet above the valley floor, the only view the snow-clad mountains on the other side of the mile-wide valley, existed a compact community that included executive bungalows with little plots of gardens, a 20-bed hospital, tennis courts, a large general store, perched on ledges on the mountain side. A little above was the main portal with a tramway that ran horizontally into the mountain to the rich ore vein. The ore, before being bucketed down to Stewart, was semi-reduced by a huge concentrating plant that sat beside the community. It was its destruction by fire that ended the operation in 1926 but the vein had been almost worked out by then anyway. Today, the torn and rust-red ruins of the concentrator and the dormitory that housed the biggest percentage of the miners are all that remain, although when we were there in '66 an operation was underway to clean up the low-grade ore that was left and to glean whatever it could from the old tailings.

The clapboard dormitory begins as a two-level structure on the "main street" level and when it has reached the level below has become a seven-storey building slanting down the mountainside. Beside it was the communal dining hall and recreation centre and while the dormitory was still upright, the hall had been smashed to firewood by the weight of winter snows. The three-foot deep steel I-beams, 50 feet long, once supporting the roof, were bent in rusty V's. Poking above the rubble was the concrete projection booth still housing a pair of mangled 35 mm. motion picture projectors.

Inside the mouldering, dank, ghost-like dormitory, gingerly treading dark, shaky stairways and threading down dim, smelly passages from which bedrooms opened, we could see the ravages of 40 years abandonment to the wilderness. Signs of rats were everywhere. Gobs of moss clung in corners and on walls in places where water dripped. Molded suitcases, slimy boots, china mugs, pulpy books, shreds of clothes still hanging in the drying room, disintegrated magazines, patches of newspapers breeze-ruffled, flapped on the walls—it was a horribly unforgettable sight and smell. It got to me, and that moment, to Helen too. Herb and Ian had disappeared down a particularly rancid passage looking for the shot they were seeking. Helen and I looked at each other and without a word hurried back to the sunshine and the clean mountain air.

Herb found his shot exactly the way it had been the year before—boots and mug on a table beside a book overgrown with moss four-inches high, set against a broken window looking out to the valley. It appeared in the book. He told me after he finished photographing the scene, he picked it all up and threw it out the window so the shot couldn't be duplicated. It wasn't any loss.

As we ate the lunch of ham sandwiches and a six-pack of beer Ian's chef had packed, sitting on a rock in the mine manager's overgrown garden, Ian told us another story. He pointed out another portal opening across the valley at about our same level where the gold ore vein had reappeared on the other side. An aerial tramway had connected the two workings with a mile-long steel cable, 3,000 feet above the valley floor. Long, flat, open-topped boxes like coffins, slung on the cable from pulleys and rode across the chasm carrying men, equipment and ore. As McLeod told it, one day an apprentice engineer was in control of the steam-powered cable hauling machinery and some men were in a "coffin" on the way across. The lunch whistle blew. The engineer shut down and went off to the dining hall to leave the men stranded and swaying over the valley. The "coffins" had 18-inch high sides and the men rode them lying flat, four to a box, covered with fur blankets. It was mid-winter and the valley wind swung the boxes in wide arcs. So the men lay rigid and petrified for a whole lunchtime hour a mile in the air. The engineer was shipped back to Vancouver on the next Union boat.

That twilight after dinner, Ian drove us up the canyon-like valley of the Bear river on the Canadian side of the ridge. This is the southern end of the publicity-prone Stewart-Cassiar road that only has a comparative few miles to construct in its centre for it to connect with the Alaska Highway and thus open a vast new section of the province for tourist and transport travel. When it is finished it will be breathtakingly scenic. Fifteen miles from Stewart, high on a mountain shelf, we stopped to gaze in awe at the Bear Glacier. Way above where the edge of the ice field showed, a great white ribbon began its inexorable overflow as it followed a gentle "S" into the valley. As it neared the bottom its surface became scarred and wrinkled and then broke into crevices 200 feet deep. A cold blue color radiated from this area. At the toe where it was melting, small ponds of water connected to become a stream that flowed off toward Stewart and the sea as the Bear River.

Next morning at 08:30, airborne off the Stewart strip, circling tight in the valley, we headed back up the Bear River canyon for a 2½ hour flight to our next stop. The weather was terrible and I thought, here's where the schedule gets shot to hell. The ceiling was low, shrouding the mountain peaks half way down into the valley. The rain was smashing on the windscreen. The ADF needle was sweeping the dial unable to get a fix on a radio range beacon, meaning we were far away from civilization. I had a feeling things would get better so I kept barreling up the valley just able to make out the walls on both sides. A half hour later it did begin to clear and in fifteen minutes we broke into sunshine right on course, as we could see by the scar of the Stewart-Cassiar road below.

That was the only sticky weather we experienced in the entire trip. It was a phenomenal summer in '65 and we hit the best part.

Our destination was 300 air miles due north of Stewart—a little piece of water in the Dease Plateau called Good Hope Lake. If you shut your eyes for a second you could miss it. From here on until we neared the coast again, I was in unfamiliar territory and I found satisfaction in chart reading and flying by the compass.

We made a greased landing on Good Hope and taxied to a small float tied to the shore. Two little Indian boys fishing from it was the only sign of life. We were five minutes ahead of our ETA made months before. I thought that damn good. "Too bad you couldn't have been on time," was all Herb said. A car came down the dirt road on the button, and the driver greeted us with a big handshake. He was the superintendent of the asbestos mine at Cassiar and he had driven 20 miles to meet us and transport us to Cassiar.

The operation is the literal removal of an entire mountaintop—6600-ft. Mt. McDame. From that rare atmosphere with the whole of the snowy Cassiar range spread in broad array, where in winter the wind-chill hits 60 to 70 below zero and the men have to work in electrically-heated huts, where gigantic shovels, trucks, drilling machines crawl around the sky, and explosives make it tremble with noise, a gray-green mountaintop of almost solid fine-grade asbestos ore supplies about 10 percent of the total Canadian production. In 1967, well over one million tons of ore produced over 90,000 tons of fibre for round-the-world sales worth over $20 millions. Preliminary mining started in 1952 and it is estimated there is about another 30 years production left. The same company has begun production at another site almost equal in size, 400 miles northwest of Whitehorse in the Yukon.

Getting the fibre to market is a major accomplishment of modern transportation. The ore leaves the mountaintop on a 3-mile long bucket tramline where at the bottom, next to the fine company town of 900 people, it passes through the concentrator. Then big trucks carry it 80 miles out to Milepost 650 on the Alaska Highway and north up the highway 250 miles to Whitehorse. There the ore is loaded into freight cars of the White Pass & Yukon railroad and brought down to tidewater at Skagway where it goes to sea on the specially-built carrier *Frank H. Brown* which finally discharges at the new Asbestos Wharf in Vancouver harbour on the North Vancouver side. From here the ore is picked up by the ships of the world as sales warrant.

We were given a bountiful lunch by white-capped chefs in the company mess and then taken up the mountain to see the workings, where Herb would get the photograph he had planned for Cassiar of the long tramline.

Late in the afternoon, we were driven back to the lake and we were airborne again at 17:30 for a short flight of 80 miles, north to Watson Lake to spend the night. Watson Lake is seven miles north of the British Columbia border, in the Yukon, on the 60th parallel. It is 770 air miles from Vancouver and we were about 450 air miles north of Prince Rupert. This was to be our most northern point. From here it would be all downhill.

The airport at Watson Lake, a mile from the Alaska Highway, was built by U.S. Army engineers solely as a stop in the staging route between the United States and Russia, at the time when Russia was an ally. This was the end of a long flight from aircraft plants in the U.S., of new fighter planes the Americans were supplying Russia at the time of the siege of Stalingrad. Russian ferry pilots picked up the fighters at Watson Lake and flew them over the top to Russia. Most of those pilots were women and they had little navigation experience. The practice was for the fighters to make the Watson Lake-Russia leg in groups of three with one navigator in the lead plane navigating for the trio. There are many reports of groups of three fighters slamming into the mountains of the Yukon and Alaska, one, two, three, as the navigators erred. In some cases, the second plane would pile into the wreckage of the first, and the third plane into the wreckage of the second, so precise was their flying, albeit at a wrong altitude or on a wrong course.

We had a hearty dinner in the old Watson Lake hotel, a low, log structure of great age that smelled of inch-thick steaks and a million logs in the big fireplace. The village is strung along the Alaska Highway— trading posts, a couple of hotels, truck depots, the RCMP post, the service yard for the Central division of the highway and some Indian houses. It was almost midnight when we went to bed but still daylight, and except for a drunk who insisted the McDonalds were in his room we spent a good night.

Early next morning, bright and clear, fuelling up to the gas caps for a long day's flight, we awaited the arrival of the CPA daily flight from Vancouver before taking off. We were airborne at 09:00 and followed the Alaska Highway back across the B.C. border as far as Lower Post, the Indian mission settlement, then striking southeast across the barren Liard Plain, headed for the Kechika river. You have seen vapor trails etched high in the stratosphere by fast, high altitude aircraft, straight as a taut string. That day, if the Beaver had been high enough, our vapor trail would have been just as straight for 346 air miles as we followed the path of the Kechika then the Finlay rivers that bottom a strange geological freak called the Rocky Mountain Trench. It is the province's most prominent lineament extending almost from the Liard river at Lower Post all the way to the Canada-U.S. border. It forms the western edge of the Rocky Mountains. From the air it looks like a bulldozer with a 20-mile wide blade and controlled by a gyro compass, had scooped out and pushed back the world's biggest, straightest, deepest ditch. From the Yukon border to half way down the province, not a road crosses it. The chart shows only wandering trappers' trails. There is no habitation in it, beside it or nearby. As you fly southeast, 4500 to 7800-foot Rockies are on the port side and the slightly lower mountains of the Ominecas are on the starboard. Down below, hour after hour, there was not a sign of life, not a plume of smoke, nothing but the muddy river flowing south to join the Peace, and trees, scrub and swamp. Every so often I would call our Vancouver transmitter and report and if I wanted to admit it, I suppose just to hear a voice from another civilization. It was strange to hear him in all that loneliness and to realize that only those in aircraft have ever seen it, at least in this modern world.

We were searching for the remains of Fort Grahame that were supposed to be on the east bank of the Finlay. My charts didn't show it but Herb's big-scale sectional maps did. He wanted a view of it for his historical chapter, from the ground if possible. The Provincial Archives in Victoria had been able to provide only sketchy information. It shows up on an old chart in the Oblate Father Morice's 1904 book *History of the Northern Interior of British Columbia*, but he does not mention it in his text and neither does Margaret Ormsby's "history". But there it was where Herb's map said it would be—a tiny, spired, leaning church, a piece of broken glass winking in the sun, a few desolated outbuildings, in a clearing on the river bank, overgrown with tall grass and scrub bushes. We flew a hundred feet over the spot and we could see it would make some good pictures of the past if we could but land in the river. After a half dozen passes up and down and not finding anything to moor to once landed, we had to content ourselves with an aerial view and press on.

We left our southeast heading and headed due

south, leaving the Trench to pick up the Omineca river a few miles west of the fork where it joins the Finlay and where the Finlay joins the Peace. The target was Germansen Landing. For his chapter on the communities of the province, from the cities of Vancouver and Victoria, through the smaller cities, towns and villages, Herb had chosen this one-family outpost to represent a remote settlement. One of the forest product industry foresters had told him about the family, and since it only received mail once a month, Herb's letter reached them June 15. It was now July 25 and we were right on schedule.

The forester had said the Omineca was wide and ran past the place so slowly in mid-summer there would be no trouble making a water-landing; that we would see a single-lane wooden bridge of many trusses crossing the river just below the little cluster of buildings; not to attempt to land ahead of the bridge. Land on the other side he had instructed, and taxi back under the bridge to a beach in front of the place.

There were the buildings and there was the bridge, on course over the bow. I went round the place low, waggled the wings and then took a long glide, skimming us over the bridge to put us into the river on the other side. Turning around, I slowly made way back to the bridge and the centre span we were supposed to slip under began to look smaller and smaller as we closed. We'll never go through that I said to myself, and had a queer idea. "Herb," I asked, "could it be that forester has always been here in a Cessna?" "Holy smoke, Justin, I dunno. I told him it would be a Beaver and he didn't say anything, that I remember." "Well by God," I said, "if we go through there my guess is we're going to end up with a new-model Beaver with stubby wings." I was slowly circling on the water in front of the span as we thought about it with some alarm. Ten minutes went by and I still hadn't made up my mind to try when a jeep with a man and boy, arrived on the bank. He laughed and said "sure looks tight doesn't it?" "You're damn right," I called, "will we fit?" "Sure," he said, "take it nice and slow and line up with that big bolt in the centre span." So, taking a bead on the prominent bolt head and moving dead slow, I think half way through I actually shut my eyes. Measuring it later, I found there had been 18-inches clearance either end of the wingtips and just a mere foot above the tail.

The Westfall's of Germansen Landing are an extraordinary family. Wes was an electronics engineer with Douglas Aircraft in California and was growing perturbed about the influence the "beat" generation was having on his children, two boys and a girl. He had made some startling contributions to the industry and his career looked promising when he suddenly resigned, sold out, loaded a jeep and headed north. He said he was going to take his family so far back of civilization and all its works the only influences exerted on his children would be what he and his wife brought them. At that time, they were about twelve, nine and seven. He drove up the Cariboo highway as far as Prince George, turned east on "16" to Vanderhoof, turned north again to Fort St. James. That still wasn't far enough and he kept going north, ever north, over 200 miles of road, almost trail, until at the end of it on the bank of the Omineca, where once there was a silver boom, he found his Shangri-La, an old trading post for sale. That was in the early '60's.

Today, with none but a few Indian families and

itinerant trappers for a hundred miles around, he is the general storekeeper, magistrate, claims recorder, notary —name it. Maggie is the postmistress. The DOT has installed a big power generator and some good transmitting equipment together with an array of weather recording instruments and Maggie is the department's official weather observer transmitting on a regular daily basis to Prince George. The children were taking the B.C. Dept. of Education's correspondence courses and were doing well. They had grown to be self-sufficient, mannerly, respectful and responsible to one another. Afterward, the McDonalds and I agreed none of us had ever met a family, collectively or individually, to impress us so much.

The old house had been almost entirely renovated It was warm, clean, bright and cheerful. Wes and the boys had built a half-dozen outside log cabins with wood heaters and good beds that are well-known by the pilots and the company executives who continually roam the hinterland in private aircraft. The store/ /office/ post office was new and so neat it looked like a museum piece. On the wall was a magnificent, super-size lynx pelt brought in by an Indian trapper in February in its prime time.

After a tour of the place, while Herb got the pictures he had planned, Maggie gave us a chef's dinner I still relish. Over coffee, I remember Wes saying: "A man spends a third of his life asleep and I wanted to spend that third with a clear conscience." If the results shown by his children were his criterion, he must be sleeping content.

Maggie had a tremendous ham and egg breakfast ready next morning and in the middle of preparing it had to run to the transmitter and give her weather report. Fine, it was. The schedule was still lucky. I had been up at dawn to hand pump 45 gallons of fuel from one of Wes's drums into HGZ and so at 08:30, we oozed under the bridge again and took off for the short 120 mile flight due east to Hudson's Hope and the Portage dam on the Peace river, now re-named the W.A.C. Bennett dam. As we landed on the asphalt strip and drew up under the shadow of a just-arrived Pacific Western Airlines flight, Bill Findlay, B.C. Hydro's project manager halted his car under our port wing.

Findlay gave us a good day, albeit a hot, dry, dusty one of atrocious driving that had us in hysterics most of the time. The concept of the Peace dam is so gigantic that even when you are looking at it you still can't conceive it. A mile and a quarter long, 600 feet high, it was at that time the largest construction project underway in the western world and there was a particular point of pride that day to realize it was entirely a provincial construction.

Herb's book said later: "Of its 1.9 million population (1967) British Columbia has only some 700,000 wage earners. That is less than half the population of metropolitan Toronto. Each of the 700,000 is contributing one thousand dollars to the $700 million first stage cost of the Peace river power development. When this is compared to the $641 millions St. Lawrence Seaway project, much of it paid from federal funds, it is no wonder British Columbians are proud, as in summer, they stand by the thousands on the edge of the Peace and watch the great machines thunder in the valley."

By the early '70's, when the river behind the dam has backed up to capacity, a lot of the Rocky Mountain Trench we had flown over would be a 240 mile long,

640 square mile lake, so big it will bring a climatic change to that area. The hydroelectric power it will generate in the world's largest underground power house carved inside the rock, will provide energy for the continuing growth of the province. In a day or two we were to see the long lines of the new power lines snaking over the hills as they were being constructed on their way south.

Findlay gave us lunch in the executive cafeteria and then showed us from a cliff lookout the mouths of three diversion tunnels where the great Peace was being diverted to dive under the mountain and come up again on the other side downriver, in thunderous spume. Then he took us four miles away to the glacial moraine where nature eons ago had thoughtfully deposited all the necessary sand, gravel and rock that was providing the 60 million cubic yards of fill for the dam. He explained the world's longest conveyor belt system that was moving the fill to the damsite at a rate of 12,000 tons an hour—so successfully, the ultimate result was that the dam part of the project was finished a year ahead of schedule. At the damsite he showed us how the tremendous belly-dumper trucks were loaded with 100 tons of fill in 30 seconds and how this work went on, 24 hours a day except for the winter season. It was a panorama of determined men and gigantic machinery.

We were off the Hudson's Hope strip late in the afternoon for the 40-mile flight to Fort St. John where Dan Murray parked his dusty station wagon by the door as the prop stopped outside the visiting aircraft hangar. "Welcome to God's country," he said. "If by that you mean a shower," Helen said, "I'll love the place." Dan left us at the Fort hotel and to our own devices, mainly soap and water, until dinner time.

Then we all went off to a new motel down the highway.

British Columbia's natural inheritance has been a 366,200 square mile tortured land of many distinct topographic areas and the people of those areas are as different as the regions. The 20,000 square mile Peace River country lying between the Rockies and the Alberta boundary, is a black-loamed prairie empire as rich on the surface as it is in petroleum under it. It houses the dangdest, toughest, most impatient frontiersmen to be found on the continent. Chief poobah, greeter, jingoist, one-man chamber of commerce, is ebullient and forceful Dan Murray, publisher of the News at Fort St. John, who each year takes off with Kay, his wife, for some place in the world to further his understanding of people and governments. He had just returned from East Berlin. In '67 it was to be Russia. The biggest mystery in life to Dan is why all the people in the world don't pack up and move to the Peace. "Heaven, that's just what it is!" he always says. It has a long way to go before it is, with its piercing cold in the bleak winters, its dust, heat and bugs in summer and its between-season mud. What he really means is that for young, aggressive men with stars in their eyes, and with guts and determination, no greater place of opportunity exists than the Peace. He could be right. It was quite a discussion that night over dinner and Dan did most of the talking.

Next morning, through Dan's arranging, we were picked up at the hotel by Bill McLaughlin, resident manager of Pacific Petroleums, and taken on a 100-mile tour north into the muskeg country to witness a diamond drilling rig at work.

The subterranean basement of the Peace is proving to be a storehouse of petroleum and natural gas energy. In 1966 the wells produced 200 billion cubic feet of gas and over 14 billion barrels of oil plus the byproducts of butane, propane and sulphur. The gas reserves have a conservative estimate of 90 trillion cubic feet and the proven reserves of oil and liquid hydrocarbons are estimated at 500 million barrels. The provincial government owns all the oil and gas lands and thus takes to its budget a big royalty which is one of the ways a small population supports a country the size of British Columbia. It isn't all black gold, as they say. Between 1951 and 1964 for instance, the major oil companies spent $600 millions for exploration and another $355 millions for production costs and royalties. To bring in the 500-odd existing wells, some 3,000 exploration holes had to be drilled totalling hundreds of miles. It was to one of these that McLaughlin was taking us, already down 3200 feet.

Before reaching the drill site we stopped at the camp which was a cluster of linked trailers—a system that has made a fortune for the inventor and manufacturer in Edmonton. Rented, and floated to the site on trucks, each trailer is fitted to form a unit of a complete complex. There are the dormitory trailers with centre corridor and nicely furnished two-man bedrooms. There are the washroom trailers with toilets, showers and basins, a laundry trailer, lounge trailer, commissary trailer and mess hall trailer, all linked together, all spotless. Two nice ladies were the cooks and brought us heaped bowls of fried chicken pieces, quantities of fresh vegetables and for dessert, with the thermometer outside showing 96 degrees, a soup tureen piled with a gallon of hard ice cream. The work is dirty but companies caught in the squeeze of labor demands, have certainly taken the roughing-it part away.

At the drill rig we found that oil companies, for the most part, no longer do their own exploratory drilling. This is done by specialist contractors who provide their own collapsible equipment which is hauled from site to site on special trucks. A rig operates with a seven-man crew working with the precision of a ballet dance team. Every man knows his job, his position and his segment of the work that when more drill pipe has to be added, is performed with split-second timing. It's either that or get killed, the way that chain flies around . We watched a stand of pipe being added—22 seconds of lightning action and flawless form.

On the way back to Fort St. John, Herb seemed in thought. I asked him what was on his mind. He said nowhere in our trip had we seen a pick-and-shovel laborer, even on the Peace dam project. The exotic tools, compared to those a few years ago, were such that while the doers could make a great deal of money these days, it took men who knew their machines, who were tough enough for the pace. It was the major lesson he was getting from the trip, he said.

We were back in town by 4 o'clock with lots of suntime left, so we cranked up the Beaver and went out over the flat farm lands for some aerial views. I pretended I was back in my crop dusting days, skimming low over the fields and pulling back for a sudden rise of trees. The fall wheat was beginning to show and the land was aglow with color. It was the end of the seventh day of our trip.

Next morning, July 30, we were on the way a few miles south to Dawson Creek where I meant to take on fuel for a flight of 310 air miles that day. There are so many float planes flying about the B.C. interior these

107

days that Dawson Creek, in the middle of a prairie, has installed its own body of water at the airport near the runways. A mile-long, 450-foot wide ditch was bull-dozed out of the surface and filled with four feet of water. It is a unique answer to a local problem but since I wanted fuel, we landed on wheels and taxied to the gas pump.

By 08:30 we were off again on a heading which paralleled the B.C.-Alberta boundary, ten miles west of it. First the flat lands, then the gentle hills that became foothills and finally, two hours south of Dawson Creek, there was the roof of the continent that is surely North America's most majestic sight.

The Rocky Mountains of British Columbia, geo-logical adolescents only 65 million years old, are still sharp and craggy with the marks of Nature's chisel still showing. Even above them at 10,000 feet, our altitude by then, their grandeur is undiminished. It is even more breathtaking because you can see them row on row to the horizon. Mt. Hanington, Mt. Ruth, Mt. Buchanan, Mt. Pauline, Mt. Renshaw, Mt. Holmes, Perseverance Mt., they passed in review, first on one side, then on the other. It was a glorious parade and its was glorious to be airborne. Even Bo wasn't asleep. He was standing on the seat watching the scene below and whuffing to himself.

Herb had the window open and was shooting rapidly. He turned and said, "Justin, we're not too far from Mt. Robson are we?" "Just a short deviation from our straight line course," I answered. "Why don't we go and take a look then," he said. "This weather is so fine it is just possible Robson may be clear from top to bottom." I veered slightly east to pass over Carcajou Pass in Jasper National Park and began reaching for more altitude. Over the top of Gendarme Mt. at 9,500 ft., Mumm Peak at 9,700 ft., across Robson Pass and there was the queenly lady dead ahead—all 12,972 feet of her, highest of all the Canadian Rockies. From her diadem of snow crest her white mantle trailed all the way to the bottom like ermine streamers from a cape. At her feet was a milk-green rug of glacial lake. I tried for more height but HGZ was beginning to feel the thin air now. Still, slowly she climbed loaded as she was with her pontoons, her big gas load and all our equipment, until at 11,100 feet the altimeter needle would move no more. We were at the Beaver's ceiling for that day, 1,800 feet below the peak. Thus we circled her, 500 feet from her snowy head. The film was running through the camera like quicksilver for it was a rare occasion. Even Bo was caught up in the excitement. I bet he's the world's only dog who has ever barked at the peak of Mt. Robson.

From here it was a long 70-mile downhill glide to pick up Valemount on the CNR line and follow it down to Blue River and its temporary asphalt construction strip on the abuilding Yellowhead Highway, our destination for the afternoon and evening. Two highway engineers rolled up in a Dept. of Highways orange car alongside the aircraft. They took us to check in at a motel, then to a cafe for lunch, then 15 miles up the new highway where heavy construction equipment was tearing up a hill and loading it into dumpers.

A few years ago, Blue River's only reason for existence was as a divisional point on the CNR's main line from Edmonton and Jasper to Kamloops and Vancouver. A road followed the railway, so bad and treacherous it was closed in winter, so hazardous it should have been closed in summer too. Only the brave tried it and those who have, talk about it as the great adventure. Now another Rogers Pass-type highway was being built on the same route and when finished it will be B.C.'s gateway from Edmonton, as the Trans-Canada–Rogers Pass route is its gateway from Calgary. It will also add new development to the country on both sides of it.

Better than half the total provincial population is concentrated in the Lower Fraser valley, housing Vancouver, and the Saanich peninsula of lower Vancouver Island, housing Victoria. The rest of the people are scattered throughout the vastness. Where the majority concentrate comes the greatest demand, yet the land they occupy is a pin prick compared to the rest of the province, equal in size to the states of Washington, Oregon, California plus 36,000 square miles of Mexico. The government has had to be a Robin Hood, taking from a rich area and giving to a poor one. If this province was to flourish it contended, it could not just tax less than a million wage earners. It had to open up the land so the rich resources could be developed. Thus, beginning in the early 50's, a highways' program was launched that each year until 1967, accounted for the major part of the provincial budget. In those 15-odd years, over $1 billion was spent on roads, bridges and maintenance. Today, B.C. has over 24,000 miles of roads and 7,000 miles are paved. There are now some 3,000 bridges that end to end would stretch 50 miles. The new arteries are doing their job, proving to be the "roads to resources" they were planned to be. The main highways, like the Trans-Canada–Rogers Pass road and the new Yellowhead road are as well, "resource" roads in themselves since they cater to the province's second largest industry, tourism, and tourism brings almost $300 millions to the province annually. I was glad to see first hand the construction of a new "resource" highway and to talk to the dedicated men who are building what has been called the finest highway system per capita anywhere in North America.

It was 98 degrees and like a blast furnace. And it was red dust. It was an unbelievable contrast to the clean whiteness and the antiseptic air of Mt. Robson a few hours before. Herb had a terrible time getting the one good construction shot he wanted although he had lots of cooperation from the crew as they moved the big shovel here and there and parked trucks just so. Dust was on everything and getting to the lenses. Herb quit after an hour of sweat but I could see he wasn't happy. As we drove back to Blue River he saw two tanned musclemen jockeying an air drill into a granite boulder and surrounded by a halo of red dust. "That's the shot," he said, and got it in a few seconds.

Next morning early, we climbed off the short Blue River strip with the big trees looming large at the end, heading due west 120 miles, for Williams Lake, centre of the Chilcotin country. Now the Rockies were gone and the green forested valleys gave way to the sparsely treed, rolling, yellow-red hills of the range country. Sea, plateau, prairie, snowy mountains, and now almost desert, I was thinking, how many faces this province has!

Williams Lake was to be only a re-fuelling stop and some coffee in the airport cafeteria, then we went down across the beef and sage country to Clinton to pick up the P.G.E. rail route to follow it to Kelly Lake. Here we circled while Herb took some views of hydro-electric power lines running across the hills. Now to turn south east and fly over Pavilion Lake and the Hat

Creek district, cross the Thompson river canyon and turn south for Merritt to find the gigantic hole in the ground—the Craigmont open pit copper mine where everything dug goes to feed the industries of Japan. Then due west again to Lytton and the junction where the Thompson river meets the muddy Fraser river, to fly down the canyon into Vancouver and to the company's home base at the airport. Pause here to drop off some no-longer-needed equipment, refuel and off again, across Vancouver and its growing spires of skyscrapers, over Lions Gate bridge to follow the shore past Horseshoe Bay with a ferry just pulling out, over Gibson's, up the sunshine coast to Powell River to glide low past one of the continent's largest newsprint paper mills. Head across Georgia Strait, Savary Island on the starboard, scattering cormorants sitting on the floating logs, watching trollers after salmon, to land in the slough behind the Spit Camp at Campbell River, one of our company's major bases. Pictures all the way. 585 air miles this day, all the way from Blue River to the sea. It was good to smell it again and feel myself in familiar territory.

Off early next morning, still in fine weather, crossing Vancouver Island, through the pass to Tahsis, company town of the East Asiatic company. Picture. Herb, the night before, had asked Tofino Radio to contact the keeper of the Nootka Light so when he heard us he would be out on the walk around the tower. Down Tahsis Inlet to the sea and Friendly Cove where British Columbia's history began, to zoom low and slow past the lighthouse a half dozen times, taking its picture while the keeper stood there and probably thought us nuts. Out over the open sea, it was good to see the broad Pacific horizon again. We glided over the breaker-beaten rocks scaring flocks of sea birds and turned north up the coastline looking for the one view depicting forest and sea and deep-running inlets. Along the beach at Kyuoquot, the Indian village, I became so wrapped up in the job, I blew a tank but wobbled gas back in time before we hit the water. Across Checleset Bay to round Cape Cook, we were tossed like a kite riding the Pacific wind. Back across the Island again to circle Coal Harbour to see if there were any whales at the station. No whales. And so to Port Hardy for lunch and to say hello to some of the boys who seemed envious of our trip. I told them they could be.

Out over the Johnstone Strait, going back to the mainland, we crossed Seymour Inlet, and then up into Boswell Inlet to a float village I knew so Herb could get his float village picture which became one of his best. Still airborne, out across Fitz Hugh Sound to Calvert Island's western side, we flew past the B.C. Telephone company's micro-wave repeater station a few times to picture it from different angles. So to Ocean Falls to trundle up the company ramp and check in at Crown Zellerbach's Martin Inn.

Next morning we went seeking a photograph that would show the fingers of fog creeping up the inlet from the ocean. Imagine trying to find fog, I thought. We found it, stayed above it and got the shot. Then down the inlet low, skimming a few feet above the sea, to find different examples of fishing boats, on a route that would bring us to Namu, the largest fish processing plant on the coast. Destroyed by fire a few years ago, it has been rebuilt to an automated state and has become a prime centre for thousands of fishermen in the area who in large majority, are Indians. The fishing industry of the coast has offered the Indian opportunity to be his own master and he has taken advantage of it. The smell from the reduction part of the plant, where the guts are reduced to expensive fish meal, was such at 3,000 feet above it, Bo started to sneeze. On the ground where Herb took his principal pictures, it was a sight of raw commerce as bloodied silver salmon in their thousands were bucketed out of the packers' holds to the platforms and shoved to the graders to be graded according to size, quality and type.

It was 15:00 hours, three o'clock of a warm, sunny, summer afternoon when HGZ, her engine still humming with heart, took us up the Ocean Falls ramp again and to the end of a 10-day magnificent trip.

To complete the story, the book appeared in November, 1966, 15 months later, under the title: *British Columbia: Challenge in Abundance.* By Christmas that year it had sold 35,000 copies and had made some Canadian publishing history. Herb had me invited to the launching luncheon in Vancouver, headed by the Lieutenant Governor, George Pearkes, and it was an auspicious day.

The schedule had us ending at Ocean Falls in the afternoon of the 10th day. I was supposed to deadhead back to Prince Rupert and my last duty was to get the camper truck out of storage and have it put into a covered barge scheduled freight run to Vancouver. It arrived there a week later, I heard, surrounded by a thousand cases of canned salmon.

So saying warm goodbyes to people who had become good friends, and with a wet lick on the ear from Bo, I winged out of Ocean Falls and headed home. It was a beautiful time of early evening. The sun was lowering into the Pacific and I was going home with a tremendous feeling of lift. My mind was full of the sights we had seen and the thoughts they had stirred. Suddenly, what was *that*? It couldn't be but it was! Only 15 miles from home and by God, after ten days of glorious weather, there was the old familiar Prince Rupert welcome—Fog!

I went down to the water, landed—and of all the ignominious endings . . . taxied the rest of the way to Prince Rupert.

Airborne
Ambulance

I HAVE OFTEN WONDERED why British Columbia, with so many thousands of people living and working in the thousands of inlets along the coast, has not begun a Flying Doctor service as Australia possesses. There the doctor is flown to the patient or the doctor flies himself. Perhaps the day will come.

In the meantime, the practice over the past 15-odd years here has been to fly the patient to the doctor. Despite the time delay (and it seems to shorten each year) the system seems to work and chances of recovery are now in the patients' favor. As the largest small-plane operator working the coast, our company, together with all the other smaller operators, has assumed the responsibility of providing ambulance service whenever needed. There is no government subsidy. It is no more than a humanistic responsibility that when a person needs help, we are duty bound to pick him up and get him to aid—and to stop everything else until the job is done.

Scores of times, a Beaver load of passengers en route to a logging camp or other point of call, is put on the ground immediately the pilot gets a radio message that there is a stretcher case in the vicinity. He lands at the nearest place, perhaps a logging camp or fishing village, beaches the passengers and heads for the patient. Another aircraft is sent to pick up the passengers and take them onward. They never object because they know next time it could be for any one of them.

Many is the time when bad weather cancels all scheduled and charter operations for the day, but if an emergency call comes, none of us think twice about making an attempt. I have flown in weather so bad it scares me even now. It was the kind DOT inspectors pick up your ticket for, if it had been attempted with a paying passenger. The name of the game is Patient and it is a code of honor among pilots and dispatchers to help in distress. No questions are asked beyond the nature of the injury, where the patient is and if an ambulance will be needed at the destination.

Our company has acquired the reputation for providing one of the world's largest airborne ambulance services and has been responsible for saving hundreds of lives over the years. In the past 15 years, 5,475 days, we have averaged a stretcher case a day. They haven't all been men injured in industrial accidents. There have been a lot of expectant mothers too, most always "just in the nick of time." Two I remember were born in the back seat of Beavers en route. Thank God neither were when I was at the controls. Taxicab drivers live in constant fear and so do pilots.

The system works so well, now an injured man from way back in the bush gets to an urban hospital sometimes faster than a metropolitan traffic accident victim to the same hospital. I recall a logger who was working in a west coast Vancouver Island operation who he was speared through the middle by a six-foot limb falling from a tree, actually pinning him to the ground. It was only a short time before he was aboard one of our aircraft and flown direct to Vancouver airport, 145 air miles away, to be in the Vancouver General hospital two hours and five minutes after the accident. In contrast, I saw an accident on the freeway not far from my Vancouver home and it took three hours to get one of the car drivers to the same hospital, only 12 miles away.

In these years of the middle sixties, the number of stretcher cases has dropped considerably, due in part to greater stress being placed upon safety education among the companies of the forest products industry. Another reason is the gradual disappearance of the gypo logger which is a particularly northwest coast handle for a logger who works for himself. He may operate a one-man show, living from a boat or a barged or rafted house, picking steep slopes close to tide-water so when he fells his trees they slide into the chuck with little help. He might have a helper or a partner or he might have 20 men working for him, but whatever the situation they are tough, rough and usually single. Their decline, corresponding to the steady growth of large company operations working from large camps or company towns with the facilities for wives and children on the site, is resulting in a better calibre of logger with regard for his safety and the safety of others.

Despite differing conditions there is still an aspect

of bush accidents that has not changed. Most coast camps shut down completely for about two weeks over Christmas and New Year's and usually the camps almost empty as the men and their families go to town for the holiday. For the first three or four weeks following re-opening, there is always an epidemic of accidents and a lot of them are airborne stretcher cases. We have assumed that company safety programs to the contrary, the time off makes the men forget their safety consciousness and it takes them at least six weeks to get it back. Except for Easter, the next holiday usually comes at May 24. Prior to it, the men seem to be using safe practices again. After it, there is another rash of bad accidents. There seems to be no answer to the human factor no matter what safety programs are put into effect.

It is a rare occasion when our company, or any other small aircraft operator, has not been paid eventually for making a mercy flight. The majority of cases are the responsibility of the employer for he is charged to see the injured person gets proper attention. When the case concerns the Workmen's Compensation Board or the Department of Indian Affairs, it becomes a simple matter of presenting a bill at a later date for services rendered. If it is a personal thing, an illness, a need for surgery, a baby to be born, a sick child, then it becomes the personal responsibility of the person or parent and although it has taken a long time to get paid sometimes, 99 percent have eventually settled up. To most, it has been a debt of honor that took precedence. One of the reasons is the realization that non-payment this time might mean non-appearance of an aircraft next time. The coast industrial operators could not survive without our service but at the same time, we could not survive without the coast operators.

When the role of aerial ambulance driver is thrust upon the pilot, suddenly he finds himself in a most responsible position. If the weather is bad, it is his decision whether or not to fly. It would be only compounding a situation if he himself crashed and a search had to be mounted leading to possible other mishaps, or if he got to the patient and then had an accident on the way to aid. This has to be weighed against a critically injured person's need for an aircraft. Then, once the patient is on board the aircraft he knows that speed is essential. As I have explained previously, on the coast there are two ways to go, the long way or the short way. The short way is over the ridge over the next valley or inlet, over the next ridge and inlet and so on—a straight line course as far as possible. The long way is to follow the channels, going 200 miles to reach 100 miles. Another factor is altitude for the higher you go the more the patient bleeds. Most of the time the pilot is alone with his stretcher case and making decisions for both of them. We are happier when a doctor or first aid man accompanies the patient for then the responsibility is shared.

I remember a case that began at Zeballos on Vancouver Island's west coast when I happened to be duty pilot at Tahsis, 10 minutes away in the next inlet. A call came requesting emergency transport to Vancouver for a young man who had just lost an arm in a mining accident. I was there within eight minutes, had the seats of the Beaver out and stowed and was ready for the ambulance which arrived at the seaplane float a few minutes later. The 23-year old lad was bleeding badly and the doctor who came with me directed I fly to Vancouver direct.

Zeballos is 175 air miles northwest of Vancouver and to fly the direct route means 7,000 foot altitude to clear the mountains of Vancouver Island by a safe margin. If I stayed low on the sea, went all the way down the west side of the Island, rounded the southern tip and then up the Strait to Vancouver, the extra time would be considerable. On the other hand, the excellent hospital at Campbell River was 45 minutes flying time away and needed only 1,500 feet altitude to get through Elk Pass.

But the doctor said Vancouver, so down the inlet from Zeballos I went, 100 feet above the water, and up into Muchalat Arm to Gold River where an en-route-Vancouver pass begins. As we went higher, the boy's bleeding worsened. He was colorless. His face was wet with sweat and his breathing was barely perceptible. The doctor tightened the tourniquet but the emergency dressing kept reddening. We were still only at 1,600 feet and an hour away from Vancouver when I turned around. "Doctor, I don't think we'll make it with him this way. Will you change your mind and go to Campbell River?" He nodded quickly and 10 minutes later we were handing the patient over to the ambulance men there.

I saw him a year later and I was surprised to find, despite his semi-conscious condition that Zeballos day, he still remembered me. He was wearing an artificial arm by then and he stuck out his good one to shake and thanked me. If we had continued to Vancouver, I thought, you wouldn't be alive.

Our Sandspit-stationed pilot took a call from the Jedway iron mine located close to the southern tip of the Queen Charlottes. A skin diver working on some long pilings in deep water, had been down too long, had surfaced too fast and was suffering from the bends. The only decompression chamber was way south in Victoria. The pilot was airborne for Jedway at once, picked up the stretchered patient who was in agony, and with a first aid man accompanying, flew a straight line course over the open sea to the north tip of Vancouver Island. He was never more than 25 feet from the water any time. He made a short re-fuelling stop at Port Hardy and then took off again, low over the Strait all the way into Victoria. That trip was 550 miles. The diver survived, only to do the same thing a second time in the same way at the same place two weeks later—and the same pilot had to repeat the same life-saving performance all over again.

A case might start out airborne but there is no guarantee it will end that way. Again the scene is the Vancouver Island west coast and the weather was terrible as usual. The pilot with his patient was making for Esperanza, a small, emergency, mission-type hospital on Zeballos Inlet. Heavy fog forced a water landing a fair distance from the destination. The pilot was able when on the water, to get out an identifiable radio message, a hard thing to do sometimes. A fast boat was sent out to grope about and see if it could find the plane in the thick fog. After a long time it almost bumped into it. The patient was transferred to the boat and with the aircraft taxiing behind, boat and plane made it to safety. Patient and pilot survived.

Not all airborne ambulance cases are successful. Too often, despite the speed and dogged persistence, patients do die—sometimes en route, some just before being picked up, some just after reaching hospital. There are other imponderables. At Rupert, I received an urgent call to pick up three fishermen who had been burnt severely by an explosion on board their seiner. The message said they had third degree burns and needed immediate hospital attention. The weather was bad and it was only a short time to dark. They were 90 miles away, meaning a 180-mile round trip. It was hopeless, but the code says 'try anyway'. I took off in the Goose and was three-quarters of the way to Butedale where they were, when I was forced to turn back. I still had 30 miles to go and I was down in zero zero in dense fog. Dejectedly, I returned to Rupert, landing well after grounding time in the darkness. I was met with the message the three men had died. It was one of my few unsuccessful rescue flights.

The point of this is illustration that regardless of the remoteness, despite the isolation, if the person or family or small community has a short-wave transmitter capable of reaching a base point somewhere, no one is alone. They may not get their mail on the date they should, a spare machinery part may not arrive when promised, or they might not get picked up on the exact hour they counted on to go into the city, but by God, they *all* know they can depend on one thing— should injury or illness come to them, anything requiring an air ambulance, dedicated men and fast machines are only minutes away in even the foulest weather.

Crossing
Hecate Strait

WHEN I REACH THE NEXT WORLD the first man I am going to look up is Captain G. H. Richards, Royal Navy, for he impresses me as a sensitive man with a sense of humor. While surveying the north Pacific coast for Britain, it was he, in 1861, who named the water between the Queen Charlotte Islands and the mainland, "Hecate Strait." If you searched through the encyclopedia for a lifetime you would find no name more fitting for that bloody miserable piece of water.

Hecate was the moon goddess, Persephone's attendant in the underworld and the Goddess of Ghosts, Witches and Wizards. She had the power to conjure up phantoms, dreams and the spirits of the dead. In the upper world she haunted graveyards and crossroads. Greek mythology is only legend now but I state unequivocally I am one who believes she has merely changed her venue to the Strait of her name. There just has to be a reason beyond the meteorological, why that passage is so treacherous both for the mariners on it and the pilots above it. Getting picked for the Hecate schedule is the same as getting the short straw or crapping out. The only thing nice I can say about Hecate and her unmentionable namesake is that she separates the men from the boys fast.

Her gnashed teeth coastlines are more often gloom-ridden than not and shrouded in fog wraiths like funeral bindings. Without even minutes' warning, her surface can be whipped to froth and turbulence by southeast gales countering opposite currents. She is known as a ships' graveyard. She is one woman I can do without.

From October to March, the southeast gales can exceed a velocity of 100 miles an hour. In spring, late summer and fall, impenetrable fog is her treachery. There is fog in mid-summer too but it usually burns off by noon, then there can be a few hours of gorgeous weather with the sea calm and the visibility unlimited. On those rare days, once airborne above Prince Rupert, the Queen Charlottes stand clear and sharp in the west.

Hecate presents such a formidable barrier, the Queen Charlottes have not developed as the sportsmen's paradise they could be and for the same reason only a few British Columbians have more than a limited knowledge of either their beauty or their potential. I will tell you about them.

First, to correct a misconception, Vancouver Island is not Canada's most western inhabited land. The Queen Charlottes are by 150 miles. They thrust so far into the Pacific ocean they are almost 700 miles farther west than San Francisco and almost 1,000 miles west of Los Angeles. Queen Charlotte islanders are the last Canadians to see the setting sun (when they can see it).

The 52nd parallel tips their southern point, and the 54th parallel crosses a few miles below the northern capes. Nearest land to nearest land, the group lies 35 miles off the islands of the mainland in the north and 85 miles off the mainland islands in the south. The water between is Hecate Strait. In mass, the islands look like an extracted tooth with a curving root. More than seventy islands comprise the group and two of them are large—Graham Island is the northern and Moresby Island is the southern. Little Kunghit Island forms the southern tip with its Cape St. James. Graham and Moresby are separated by a skinny strip of water called Skidegate Channel running from the open Pacific on the west to Hecate Strait on the east. What hills there are average from 1,400 to 2,700 feet and the high point is Mt. Needham at 4,000 feet. The land is rock and forest, inlets, lakes and muskeg, tall trees above and some mineral wealth below.

Another Royal Navy surveyor, Capt. George Dickson, named them for his ship the *Queen Charlotte* in 1787. Now, almost 200 years later, only about 7,000 people populate the islands and less than a quarter of them are Haida Indians who cling to their ancestral home. It was on Graham Island the world famous black stone argillite carvings originated, sculptured by the Haida. To the sorrow of collectors, only three Haida are carving now, with the result that a 10-inch totem has an approximate $300 value. Their ancestors learned the art from visiting seamen in the early 1800's who furnished them with their first steel knives.

The warm Pacific Japanese current has provided a moderate, pleasant climate, albeit a wet one, and the people have become almost web-footed as they follow their daily work, mainly as loggers, miners or fishermen. A fourth industry is the recovery and packaging of peat moss. Begun recently, it is being exported as far as California as an aid to gardening. Although gold and copper were discovered just after the turn of the century, mining did not become active until the 1950's. In '61, Jedway Iron Ore Ltd. went into production near the south tip; in '67, Falconbridge Nickel Mines Ltd. opened up its iron ore reserves at Tasu on the western coast where it is estimated there is 40 years' production.

Fishing has declined, principally due to the large processing and flash freezer fish plants now established on the mainland. The one exception is at Masset where Queen Charlotte Cannery processes succulent crab and clams. Its fast frozen whole crab, in Queen Charlotte–labelled poly bags, are sold for good prices in Los Angeles' famous Farmers' Market. The Masset operation provides a lot of work for the Haida of the nearby reservation, and is a buyer for their fish and shellfish.

Logging, until mining gets into full production, is still the economic mainstay. The great virgin stands of 250-foot, 300-year-old timber growing only feet apart from the mossy forest floor provide work for over 1,000 men. Those same forests provided all the spruce that built the famous Mosquito Bomber during World War II. Today's newer generations, used to shiny, aluminum-skinned aircraft, perhaps would not know the Mosquito's skin was three-layer spruce plywood, only 1/32-inch thick. Most of it was made at a Fraser river plant near New Westminster by a process that for that time was an industrial breakthrough. Today, most of the timber cut is Douglas fir, western red cedar and hemlock.

The Hudson's Bay Co. put a few deer on the islands in 1900. In 1912, the B.C. Game Commision added another 13. With no natural predators, the deer have so multiplied they are now as populous as dogs on a city block. The islands are nearly overrun with them and residents may hunt them all year round. To have a freezer full of venison is common on the Charlottes. Elk were introduced in '29 and they number more than 60 now but they are protected.

Until the late 40's, the islanders used coastal ship services to get to and from the mainland and it was a passage that was dreaded by all. Now all transportation of people, mail and a great deal of freight uses aircraft. Thousands of passengers a year now use the scheduled air services or the extensive charter facilities. The daily service of CP Air from Vancouver to Prince Rupert, touches down at Sandspit just before landing at Rupert. Our company provides the shuttle service out of Sandspit, to the mining centres, logging camps and fishing villages, using amphibian Beavers and Grumman Goose flying boats. As well, we operate a year-round schedule between Prince Rupert and points on the Charlottes, including Sandspit, only of course, in VFR conditions. In this case VFR means: when you can see the water!

That returns me to Goddess Hecate again, miserable, treacherous and black-hearted. I'll tell you a secret—she even has her own queer ornithologic harbingers no one has seen before, at least to my knowledge.

It would be a dreadful day. The sea down below would be churning up mountains of spume in all directions but there in the middle of Hecate, always at the same spot—so much the same spot you could navigate by it—would be those small, nondescript brown birds that never flew. I have never seen them fly but they sure as hell can swim. Did you ever have a bird just sit and watch you go past, turning his head to match your pace? These do. When you fly over a flock of sea birds they dive or they take off in all directions. Not these. They just sit there like clots and watch. I've tried deliberately flying low over the big flock, but they don't budge. Many a fisherman sitting beside me in the co-pilot's seat, has insisted they are cormorants. They are not cormorants. I've looked up all the books on ornithology and they aren't in any of them. I've named them my kookybirds.

I remember another day when the weather was terrible. (The real trick is to remember when the weather was good.) In the early afternoon, a south-easterly gale had caused rough water at Masset. The agent there advised by radio he was down in misty rain with winds of 50 mph gusting to 70. My Masset passengers had been stashed in the hotel at Sandspit for the night so I left for Rupert direct in hellish conditions. I held my course on the north leg of the Sandspit radio range in awful visibility at an altitude varying from 100 to 200 feet. When I was away from Sandspit 15 minutes, my estimated ground speed was 200 mph and I was requiring 22 degrees deviation for wind drift. The wind velocity was 70 mph. Forward visibility was a half to three-quarters of a mile and below was foaming, wind-swept sea. Gusts would shake the Goose violently and I could see the increasing anxiety of my lone passenger as he cinched his seat belt ever tighter.

"Look at all those crazy birds!" he exclaimed suddenly. There they were, the kookybirds, a 600-strong flock riding about in a maelstrom as though it was a picnic.

I landed in Prince Rupert after a 27-minute flight —one of the fastest I have ever made across Hecate. I was completing my log when PWA's Goose came up the ramp. The pilot, Bob Moul, came into the office.

"Did you just get here from the Charlottes, Justin?"

"From Sandspit in 27 minutes. Fastest yet."

"Did you see those damn birds out there?"

"First time you've seen them? Those are my kookybirds."

"Sure never saw anything like those before. They were actually watching me like I was some kind of nut."

So you see, I'm not making them up.

Hecate's phantom fog is another aspect of her despicable nature. Some days I would start away from Prince Rupert by taxiing out of the harbour for 10 miles to get out of the fog, then take off and complete the trip normally. Then there was the chance the fog would still be there when I returned, with a subsequent delay in arrival time. The other hazard to this circumstance is the area's hundreds of fish boats which carry on in thick fog without reducing speed. Most of the boats are equipped with depth sounders, some have radar, and the knowing skippers navigate well with the aids. Radar sees ahead on the surface. A depth sounder probes below to the bottom and if you know the bottom you can navigate by depth sounder in blackest night like it was high noon. At the same time, a big taxiing flying boat looming out of the fog just ahead, could scare just as much hell out of the fisherman as his boat could scare the hell out of me. Directional navigation aids are designed for best performance while airborne.

I was barreling across the Strait with a full load of passengers picked up at Masset, when just about where the kookybirds were, I ran into the first wisps of ominous fog. The latest weather report was sketchy because the radio receiver was not working well that day, and as well, the automatic direction finder seemed intermittent. It would not hold steady on the Rupert beacon.

First mainland contact point is Triple Island and despite the visibility I went by it at 300 feet, right on course. I called Prince Rupert but did not get an acknowledgement. Assuming my transmitter was working anyway, I gave my position and estimated arrival there in 12 minutes.

While the fog was thick, forward visibility varied as I passed through thick and thin sections. As a precaution, I had lowered the wing floats, reduced the airspeed to 110 mph and had applied 30 degrees of flaps. I was confident I could pick up Digby Island, go round its southern tip and get into the main channel leading to Prince Rupert harbour.

But . . four minutes from Digby, the automatic direction finder needle began wavering erractically and packed up. Then the audio range sound in my earphones cut off. Both instruments going dead at the same time in fog, is like suddenly going blind in sunlight. There was only time to check the directional gyro with the compass before plunging headlong into a solid wall of fog with full flaps at an altitude of 50 feet.

A moment later I was on the glassy calm water, but the interval between touchdown at 85 mph. and when the ship mushed to a full stop seemed an eternity. If any fishboat had loomed up in that time I would have been helpless and so would the skipper. Both of us would have been write-offs.

With engines idling, the first action was to check

out the radios. Everything was so dead the indication was a master circuit breaker malfunction. I checked but it was in order so I assumed the problem was in the remote control cable leading to the sets in the stern.

I cut the engines and went aft through the cabin, telling the passengers I had radio difficulty but would be underway in a minute. There was nothing defective back there so as I went forward again I told them to prepare for a long taxi ride into Rupert.

As I fired up the engines, I saw the directional gyro spinning furiously. That was normal in the circumstance but it made the instrument useless. I still had the compass but as I have said, it is not reliable except in the air.

In the meantime, water currents had swung the ship about and I seemed headed southeast. Under power, I brought her around to a heading of 068 degrees. That, I thought, will bring me close to the south end of Digby Island. Calculating the flying time from Triple Island, including the time on the water, I estimated I should be no more than a mile or two from the island—a 15 to 20 minute taxi run.

Forty minutes later I was still taxiing, my nose almost touching the windscreen, because the fog was so thick I could barely see my turned-on wingtip lights 18 feet away. I had never seen fog so impenetrable.

I stopped the engines to clamber through the companionway and open the nose hatch. Standing there, half outside the hull, I hoped I might hear waves against rocks or any sound that would yield a bearing. Fog muffles sound but I was sure there was water lapping on a shore to port. Again in the cockpit, I headed that way slowly and periodically I cut the engines to peer and listen from my sliding window.

Suddenly there was a half-submerged reef and I had to veer sharply to miss it and just as suddenly to lose it again. I taxied another three minutes on the old heading then stopped the engines and went to the nose hatch a second time. Then I heard the distinct rattling of locks and the splash of oars.

Just as I called, a weatherbeaten herring skiff almost banged the port wing float. There was blank astonishment on the fisherman's face. Silence. Quietly, I said "Hi."

No answer. He seemed stunned. He slowly pulled himself along the wing until he was beside me at the bow.

"All my radios are dead including the automatic direction finder and I had to land some miles out. I think I'm close to the south tip of Digby Island. Am I?"

Slowly his head went from side to side. He spoke finally. "Where ya headed?"

"Prince Rupert."

Silence. Side to side again. "Sure can't reach Rupert headin' this direction."

"Stay right there," I told him, and scrambled back to get the charts. Spreading them on the bow hatch I asked him to show me our approximate position. He pointed to the narrow entrance leading to Port Edward, south of Prince Rupert. "Here ya be, son," he said.

Now I knew I was a mile south of Digby Island. As I was thanking him, he was pushing himself off and by the time I returned to the cockpit he had been swallowed by the fog.

There were some five miles to taxi but now I knew where I was. Slowly, with no difficulty, and thankfully encountering no boats, I was on the base ramp an hour later. Several of the female passengers were sobbing in relief but trying to appear nonchalant. I apologized for the delay and as I climbed out I descended into a group of RCMP, DOT, our harried dispatcher and my engineer.

"Where in hell have you been?" they said in unison. "Two and half hours ago you were going to be here in 12 minutes."

"Simmer down." I said, "Later. First get a radio-man and fix those bloody radios. The HF, the VHF, the ADF and the LF. They're all out. This aircraft is grounded."

The explanation concerns our major problem with water-borne aircraft and their constant exposure to salt-laden moisture. It makes lives of engineers unbearable for despite all their tricks and precautions designed to stop water seeping to intricate electronic equipment, they are never able to keep ahead. In this case, moisture had accumulated in the neoprene sheathing that covered the radio cable from the cockpit controls to the sets in the stern and had finally shorted out the cable system. The ship was grounded for three days while new cables and sheathing were installed and from then on all radios worked perfectly.

Passengers used to say we were wizards to find the way across Hecate without getting lost in the weather. Some would say afterward they were convinced we had been flying in circles and they were surprised when we landed where we were supposed to land. There was no wizardry except Hecate herself. It was only the application of ordinary horse sense to the basic principles of navigation. Visibility might be poor but because of certain conditions the flight could carry on in safety. There were other days when visibility would be better but because of another batch of conditions it was smarter to go home, if not stay in bed. To navigation and common sense there was another factor—a thorough knowledge of every contour of the area.

But Hecate is different because the only poor weather reference is the water and that has no pattern. By using the available navigation aids, the nondirection beacons at Rupert and on the Charlottes, and the Sandspit radio range, there is an aerial highway.

Flying a radio range is like driving an arrow-straight highway from A to B. If you veer off you are on the bumpy gravel shoulder. Radio range is the same. If you keep the audio hum in your headphones at a certain pitch, and the pitch remains constant but continues to get louder, it means you are on the radio range leg and approaching the station. A magnetic heading is combined with the radio range leg and the combination of the two makes it simple to stay on the straight and narrow.

The flight going west from Prince Rupert to Masset is another matter. There is no radio range beacon at Masset sending a signal toward you. The beacon is at Rupert and is now behind you. Masset's compass heading, when you are pointed away from Rupert, is 242 degrees magnetic. All you do therefore, is maintain a 242 degree course and at the same time keep your automatic direction needle pointing backwards at 180 degrees. So simple even you can do it.

But don't forget this is black-hearted Hecate you are crossing. Suppose there is a southeast wind. Your aircraft is going to drift with it. Now you have to counteract the drift by allowing a certain number of degrees course variation to correspond to the wind's velocity. That is the tough part only experience and thorough local knowledge can provide. Before leaving

Rupert for Masset you first check the wind velocity and the direction and then allow the correction degrees. Most of the time it is between three and seven degrees. If the wind is a moderate southeasterly, you allow about six degrees for drift and then you subtract that from the 242 magnetic heading. Now your heading is 236 degrees. You fly on this heading for four or five minutes then resume the original heading at 242, and providing the automatic direction needle is still pointing at 180 directly behind you, you are on course.

Now I'll throw another curve, as they say. Up to now you have been piloting a twin-engine Goose flying boat with all sorts of radios and direction finders and backup sets in case of failure. Do the same thing in a small Cessna or a Beaver.

In a Beaver, even on a dead calm day, your heading will be 240 degrees, not 242. This allows two degrees of drift and in all likelihood will bring you over the Charlottes, crossing the arc of Rose Spit, the Charlottes' most northern tip. If there is a wind for which you would normally provide 8 degrees correction, you add another two degrees, giving 10 degrees of drift. You might cross the Spit a little further south than you intended but at least you won't miss it altogether and end up in Japan!

With this in mind I'll tell you another fog story. It deals with a Beaver flight from Masset to Prince Rupert.

When I took off from Masset in sunshine it was my understanding Rupert was clear but a great fog bank lay low over the middle of Hecate. On reaching it I climbed above it and was in the clear at 3,000 feet. I could see across the layer of fog clear to the mainland mountains and so I proceeded merrily on the right heading experiencing no difficulty in lining myself up with the familiar mountain silhouette.

Reaching Rupert, I found the fog had spilled away from the Strait engulfing the harbour. It was socked in tight. I radioed the base and got word there was visibility under the fog and the ceiling was 1,000 feet.

I turned 180 degrees and headed back over Hecate, flying past Stephens Island whose peak was above the stratus, until I was in the clear again. Then I got the message that Masset was down in fog and so was Sandspit, the alternate. That is when you start feeling you are the loneliest guy in the world. The job to be done now was to get to the water where there was some forward visibility and fly home under it. As many times as I have done it I still never liked it. If you are trained as a VFR pilot you don't go IFR suddenly.

I went into the fog at 3,000 feet altitude and began a long descent at 500 feet a minute on a certain heading. Five minutes later I was at 500 feet and I still couldn't see the water. I reduced the letdown to 200 feet a minute and at 100 feet altitude found the water for the first time. Now I reversed the heading and started for Prince Rupert again, reducing speed and lowering the flaps. Finally, after a bit of trickery around Stephens Island, I managed to get into the harbour and back to base. I didn't like the experience.

The nuttiest Hecate fog experience I remember was on the same Rupert-Masset run when I had four passengers. It was a queer kind of fog—banks of it in patches across the water with great piles of stratus and alto stratus here and there. By twisting and turning, over the top of some, under and through others, climbing to 5,000 feet to get above yet another layer, I managed to squirm my way two-thirds across the Strait.

Then I reached a solid wall.

It was 12,000 feet high if it was a foot. Its edge was cut as though with a knife and it stretched north and south as far as I could see. I've never seen anything so sharp, so solid, so high and so long. It was like a sliced marshmallow. I knew I couldn't climb over it so I tried to go underneath. I went inside for a few seconds but it was like going into a closet and shutting the door. It was so dense in there and so thick above, no daylight penetrated. I got out fast and in the open again I radioed Masset. He said he was in the clear and couldn't understand the predicament. I made several tries to penetrate the cliff but I was like a fly trying to go through a glass window. To hell with it, I said to myself. Back to Rupert.

By this time I was 50 minutes out of Rupert. The way back was crazy. Over a layer, under a layer, around the north end of one and the south end of the next. Once I went up to 10,000 feet to get over the top of a bank and for an hour I went up and down a narrow trough between layers, unable to go anywhere except keep moving until a thin place showed up. This is the time when you bless the inventor of the automatic direction finder. The manoeuvering I was doing had taken me way off the radio range beacon highway into faraway fields but the direction finder needle was still pointing back to base no matter how I manoeuvered. I found a break, squeezed through and found I was in another layer, and so it went until Digby Island appeared. From there it was easy. I had been four hours airborne. I was handing out the passengers apologetically when the last one paused on the step, looked about, turned to me puzzled and said: "Masset's sure changed since the last time I was here."

In case you still don't understand the point about Hateful Hecate yet, maybe this one will do it:

She was her usual dreadful self that morning and I had five passengers for Masset on the regular schedule. I delayed an hour, then I delayed another hour. Three of the passengers said it was imperative for their business they get there so after another delay and feeling a weather break was coming, I took off. Reaching Triple Island, the last of the mainland points, I ran into severe squalls and was forced to get down to sea level to find a smoother ride. There I began to pick up ice and ice and flying boats don't go together. In extreme turbulence, both outside the ship and inside among the passengers, I returned to base. Two of them accepted their return sensibly. The business trio were livid.

They walked across to the competition and it was stupid enough to charter them a Cessna 180. I made it my business to tell the pilot what to expect and tried to dissuade him, but off they went. I'm glad he made it but I ran into two of the trio later and they apologized for their behaviour. They said they had flown in terrible conditions up and down the coast but had never known anything like that trip. For a time they never expected to reach Masset. One of them maintained for a time they flew upside down.

Maybe Hecate knows what she's doing. Maybe she wants to keep the Queen Charlottes to herself and this is her way.

She can be a real bitch when she wants to be and I'm glad I'm done with her!

Hangar Talk

I HAVE LOST COUNT of the number of times my wife or one of the other wives at a party has said, not without exasperation: "Look fellas, you've been flying all day. Do you have to fly all night too? It's two in the morning. For heaven's sake let's go home!"

Hangar talk is a fascinating pastime. Fishermen swap lies. Golfers swap lies. Hunters swap lies. Not airmen—they don't have to because the stories they tell when they get together in the camaraderie of men who love their jobs are so far out they could only be true. Times are changing and the era I know is being replaced by an increasing sophistication that is reducing the personal touch and easy familiarity we had with passengers. So before it's too late, I want to get on the record some of the bull session stories I remember best. They are all true.

Bill Waddington, known the length of the coast,

tells a story about Jim Lougheed piloting a Sea Bee up the route of the Pacific Great Eastern railway between Squamish and Lillooet. Over a bump in the track called McGuire, the engine quit and in that precipitous country the only place he could set down was on the rail line. He left his wheels up to make a belly landing, first touching the tracks 50 yards south of the station. Then he slid smoothly along the tracks, whipping by the station where two cronies were playing checkers. They were accustomed to the P.G.E. freights going by at 15 miles an hour, for this was the P.G.E.'s steam engine days. Afterward it was told by them that when the Sea Bee Express went by the window, one looked at the other and said "what the hell train is that?" From the keel marks on the rails, it was found that Jim's wingtip had missed the station by two inches. Beyond two lovely gouges in the bottom of the hull where he had slid on the rails, the ship was undamaged. It was taken apart, shipped back to Squamish on a flat car, reassembled there and flown to Vancouver. Jim was one of B.C. Airlines' original pilots.

Bill Sylvester was the company originator. His father had been in the feed and grain business but stubbornly refused to have anything to do with gasoline when the motor car began replacing the horse. Bill had a U-drive outfit in Victoria before the war but felt the flying era was coming. He was becoming serious about a girl who lived at Forbes Landing on Lower Campbell Lake, over 100 miles north. At the same time, she was showing increasing signs of interest in a young pilot of Canadian Pacific Airlines who also had his own plane. He would fly in, pick her up and take off for a remote lake for the day. This got Bill so mad he studied for his licence, and afterward began the same manoeuvre. They married eventually, but more importantly, Bill says, the situation forcing him into flying was the real beginning of B.C. Airlines which he organized in 1943. All his men went to the RCAF and only George Williamson returned. Bill still has the No. 1 ticket, dated December 2, 1945, for $26.40 for a short flight out of Victoria.

He tells a story of a flight from Vancouver to Bute Inlet to pick up a passenger who wanted to go to Port Alberni. After stowing him aboard, he was nicely on the step ready to lift off when he hit a big deadhead. An instant later, the ship was upside down in the water, 150 yards from shore, four miles from where the glacier's water enters the inlet. It was 11 in the morning. He managed to get a couple of life jackets out of the cabin. He was wearing an old flying suit and jacket and Air Force fleece-lined boots. Sitting on top of the overturned crate, they weren't too worried because they knew the boat that worked the camp on the inlet was on its way up from Stuart Island and would rescue them. The boat appeared on schedule but didn't see them despite their shouting and arm-waving for by this time the aircraft was low on the surface and the passenger, who was sitting on one of the spreader bars, was up to his waist. About eight o'clock that night, black and blowing, Bill saw the red and green port and starboard lights of an approaching boat. He had some mail in his pocket, lit it and held it high but there was no sign the little flame was seen. Next he lit a couple of freight manifests, then he opened his wallet and starting with the one dollar bills, began lighting them and holding them up. He was on this last $10 bill when the boat headed in their direction. The story was featured by Ripley in his "Believe It or Not" series.

Another story Sylvester tells is about a flight to

Moses Inlet, located in Rivers Inlet, to pick up the body of a man. It was his first time into that country and he took a day and half to find the place in a two-seater Fleet Canuck. When he arrived he was told they hadn't been able to keep the corpse any longer and had sent it to Ocean Falls on the fantail of fishpacker. Bill headed for Ocean Falls, going down low to check every fish-packer he saw on the way, and he finally ended up on the ramp in front of the Martin Inn there to find the RCMP with the body. There was no embalmer there then and it was decomposing rapidly. A stretcher wouldn't fit into the little machine so Bill tore off the canvas front of the luggage compartment, strapped a couple of planks to the longerons, slipped the body in feet sternward, the head almost in Bill's lap, covered with a blanket. He took off and got as far as Alert Bay to take on some fuel and then was able to make Forbes Landing before dark, to moor at the end of the 500-foot long dock, a good distance from the lodge, where Bill spent the night. He had a few drinks that evening and he had to open his yap with: "Guess what I've got in my airplane, etc.", so the guests all went down to see and the lodge owner gave him hell. At four in the morning, he decided he'd better get out of there fast and when he was still 300 feet from the aircraft, he found the smell getting strong. He lit a cigar, found it wasn't enough, so he lit a second and puffing away at both of them, he flew back to Vancouver, the air so thick with smoke in the cabin he could barely see. The RCMP met him with a hearse and were pretty per-turbed at the condition of his freight because it was five days old by then. He said it took weeks to rid the little plane of the odor.

George Williamson, who is now a B.C. Hydro

pilot, was flying a Sea Bee in the Charlottes in '47, when he hit a floating log during a landing and put the ship on the beach. Sylvester says Williamson went to a building supply store, bought a sack of cement, mixed up a gooey lump, plastered it down in the hull to fill all the holes, waited for it to set, and flew back to Vancouver. "That's the way it was done in those days," Bill said, "there were no engineers so you fixed it any way you could because the main idea was to get it back to base somehow where a new part could be fitted."

Although I wouldn't trade places, I do get a twinge of envy when I watch a jetliner captain, aloof and sparkling, walk away from his shiny ship surrounded by a chattering court of officers and stewardesses to settle into taxis and be whisked I know not where—probably to some languorous lounge filled with canapes and cocktails. Chee, I think, Boy, that's living! The envy is strongest when I am pulling myself, clammy wet, out of the cold Pacific.

Watching a pilot head for the water from his drifting aircraft is like starting at the back to read a detective story. There is no suspense. The ending is obvious from the moment he starts to go. I remember a summer twilight in Tahsis and Axel was making a routine docking in a light breeze that was blowing directly away from the float. He had delayed only a couple of seconds in getting a line attached to the aircraft, and in that time the wing strut wandered out of reach. He grabbed the trailing edge of the wing but wasn't able to exert pressure without puncturing the Norseman's fabric. Al, Lyle and I were a hundred yards away and we ran to help but by this time the ship had drifted further and Axel was leaning at a 60-degree angle, his hands clutching the wingtip, his toes hooked to the dock rail, that unhooked just as we reached him. There he was, slipping out into the inlet, hanging to the wingtip, his feet drawn up out of the water. As we knew he would, he had to let go and the splash as he went down was great indeed. All that was left of him was his cap floating on the surface, which he ignored when he came up to swim frantically after the runaway. The episode lasted 20 seconds but it has remained in my mind like an old time movie comedy.

There was another day at Butedale on the mainland, 112 miles south of Prince Rupert. It was November, cold and blustery and I was late. To save some minutes, I skimmed round the point and landed on the water in the partial shelter of the cove, with the result no one heard me coming and there was no one at the dock. A Grumman Goose, with no rudder like a seaplane, is steered with one or both engines. The approach to the float looked perfect as I cut the engines, ran aft, opened the passenger exit hatch expecting to be able by then to step to the dock. To my horror I found a gust of wind had swung the ship and it looked like the tail surfaces were going to hit the high dock. Out of the hatch, up on to the stern of the fuselage I went, nearly tripping over the ADF antenna. I hurdled that and made a leap for the horizontal stabilizer for from there it would be easy to jump down on to the dock. In the middle of my leap, I banged my nose on the almost invisible antenna wire strung from the wing tip to the tip of the fin. The shock threw me backward into the water on the far side of the aircraft. The cold water cleared my head and in desperation I grabbed for the tiedown ring on the stern, somehow keeping the tail from pranging. The salt water had started to make the blood flow fast and I wasn't seeing clearly. At that moment my lone passenger, a toothless Indian woman at least two axe handles across, waddled out of the ship through the hatch to the planking. Hearing my splashing she looked around and with no emotion asked what I was doing down there in the water. With bloodied eyes, gasping for air and still clinging to the aircraft, I couldn't think of an apt reply. She obligingly held the ship while I climbed up on the slimy, barnacled fender log, then to the dock. Watching my cap go drifting across the cove, I patiently handed out her things and without even a goodbye, she rolled away. Shivering with cold, it was a miserably sodden 45-minute flight back to Rupert. I saved the airplane, ruined my watch, lost my cigarettes and my cap, damn near died of pneumonia, lived with two black eyes for a long time and carry a scar on my nose to this day. I was a bloody awful sight when I got home.

Long legs like mine have their advantage in my kind of flying, like the leap we used to make from one pontoon to the other of a Norseman seaplane. The leap allowed you to get across without scrambling through the cockpit and over any passengers, but there was a trick to it because in the six-foot leap you had to keep one hand on one of the blades of the tri-bladed propellor. I demonstrated this once to a friend who though shorter, thought he would try. I warned him not to let go of the propellor at all costs. He made a mighty leap and immediately realized he wouldn't make it. He grabbed for the propellor and wrapped both arms around it which slowly swung to a vertical position. Then with arms and legs wound tightly around the blade he slid slowly down the shining prop to plop into the chuck. He never tried it again.

I remember a bitch of a day in Port Hardy. Flying

had been spasmodic because of heavy snow squalls. Pacific Western's flight to Vancouver was due to depart in an hour, when our dispatcher got a call from Port Alice, site of Rayonier's pulp and paper plant, to pick up seven passengers for the PWA flight—a half hour return job. Bill in a Beaver, and Grant in a 180, took off in light snow. It was about 25 above zero. The staff and some of us pilots were yakking in the dispatch room when about 40 minutes later, Bill came in with a grin, hardly able to contain himself. A few minutes later Grant hobbled in, his left side caked with ice, so shivering he was unable to speak clearly. Tommy, the dispatcher, got out a bottle of rum and on the pretext Grant needed warming up, we went off to the pilots' room and the party was on. Flying was finished for the day anyway.

"Grant landed in the 180 at Port Alice a few minutes before I did," Bill began. "You know how short the dock is over there, and I hoped Grant would get well up leaving some room behind him for the Beaver. He looked as if he was going into it pretty hot and I was right on his tail. I was out of my ship and to the dock and was able to keep the Beaver from chewing up his tail surfaces as my prop hadn't stopped completely. At that minute, the door of the 180 flew through the air, landed on the dock and skidded among the passengers who had to jump away. In his hurry to scramble from the still moving 180, Grant had shoved the door open with such force he tore it from the hinges."

"Go to hell, Bill," said Grant in the corner.

"He tied his ship down," Bill went on, "and sort of looking foolish, threw the door into the rear of the machine. I couldn't resist it. 'Hell, Grant,' I said, 'that's nothing. The other day the right wing fell off.' That did

147

it. All seven passengers made a scramble for my Beaver and climbed aboard, leaving Grant to bring back the luggage. 'That's right, folks,' I said, 'the door and wings don't fall off a Beaver.' As I cast off from the dock, Grant was loading the last of the baggage and he flew back in the snowstorm without a door."

Roy Reaville told us of a time when he was stationed at Campbell River in the middle '50's, and after watching a solid blanket of fog for a couple of hours, he and Gary Borgford decided to try to get out of it and up to Forbes Landing from where they could continue with any flying the area needed. In their 170's, they went to either end of the taxi strip on the river. Roy took off first and in about 30 seconds was through the 150-foot thick layer, on top in sunshine. Gary came on the air: "Are you out of it Roy?" he asked. "Sure, it's fine up here," Roy told him, "come ahead." So Gary took off in the opposite direction, went through the fog, found Roy and together they flew up to Forbes Landing. Later, Gary told Roy what a cinch IFR flying was. Nothing to it, he said. I just kept the needle and ball in the centre and out I came. I sure am going to practise more of that. Then they checked the aircraft and found the needle and ball instrument wasn't even hooked up.

That same day, Bob Langdon had taxied on the water under the fog, to Menzies Bay, where it was supposed to be clear. In the Beaver he had with him Al MacPherson, an engineer. He taxied so long he blew a tank and the ship started drifting about in the eddies and whirlpools of the bay, close to the Seymour Narrows outlet. After he had switched to another tank, he couldn't get started again and a check proved a dead battery. He told Al to climb out and start cranking, but Al, who couldn't swim, wouldn't budge until Bob found some rope and tied it around him. Al cranked and cranked, Bob holding on to his end of the rope, and when the engine fired, Bob was so busy trying to maintain revs he didn't give Al much chance to get back in. Al slithered his way down the pontoon and tried to climb in the co-pilot's door but there was that damn rope around his waist going all the way around under the aircraft and back into the pilot's door. Half in, half out, he kept screaming at Bob to let go his end of the rope but Bob was too busy manoeuvering in the fast tide rip. Bob finally gave him some slack and then suddenly seeing a clear spot, took off with Al still struggling to get up into the open door. They were half way to Forbes Landing, under the fog, before Al got all the way in and was able to pull the rope in after him.

Roy was impatient for Bob to finish because he had just remembered another "Gary" story about his IFR flying. Roy said that Gary was returning to Campbell River from the west coast of the island and when he came into the hangar he announced proudly he'd just flown the whole distance IFR. The fellows looked out the window and the weather was CAVU—clear above visibility unrestricted—so they said 'sure you did, anybody could today.' "I did too," Gary said indignantly. "I took off my jacket and hung it across the windscreen and I flew back not able to see a damn thing ahead." That was Gary's idea of flying IFR.

Bill Cove told the tale of flying up from Alert Bay one day when Johnny Boak, airborne from Vancouver in a Mallard, radioed him asking Bill what it was like getting across from False Head over the hump into Rupert Arm. The weather was poor in light snow so Bill suggested Johnny follow him through as soon as

Johnny got to False Head and he would lead him into Rupert Arm. Johnny acknowledged and Bill started through, but when the weather turned rougher, he called Johnny again telling him to hold, that he was turning around and going back. There was no answer but he reversed his heading anyway. All of a sudden the Mallard went screaming by him. Johnny called him a minute later. "Where are you Bill?" "I'm still circling False Head," Bill replied. "What in hell are you doing there?" Johnny asked. "It's fine here, come on over." So Bill followed Johnny over the pass instead of Bill showing Johnny how to get through.

Stu Spurr added his story about a time when he first joined the company and hung around the office a lot, observing how things operated. He noticed a little red disc hanging on the wall and for days he wondered what it was until his curiousity got the better of him and he asked Norm Kievell, the chief dispatcher. Norm told him it was the most important piece of an aircraft's equipment and carried on in that vein for awhile until he broke down and told Stu he was to take it with him any time he had a stretcher maternity case. He said it was a small clamp for clamping the cord. Stu said if he ever had such a flight he was just going to keep looking straight ahead.

Roy was reminded of a rush flight out of Toba Inlet with a woman who was about to have her baby momentarily. He had to fly her to Powell River, it was near dark, he was young, this was his first such experience, a 170 is small for the occasion, and he was scared. More than scared, he was petrified he wouldn't be able to reach Powell River before dark and he would have to spend the night on the beach, possibly practicing midwifery before dawn. He did make it though, with the

170 up to the last notch, and he was met at the dock by an ambulance and attendants. The child was born as he stood outside. "I didn't do anything," he said, "but stand around and hand the attendants things as they made the delivery in the back seat."

Stu added another story about the time after he had worked his way up through the different aircraft and was now flying a seven-passenger Norseman. He was talking to Russ MacKinnon one day telling him of some of the places he had taken the Norseman and of some of the spots he didn't think were safe because of the small size of the body of water. Russ asked him if he had ever landed or taken off in Kyuoquot Bay. "Sure," Stu said, "I've come out of there with three on board." "Hell," Russ said, "I've taken off there with seven." "Seven!" Stu exclaimed, "the hell you did! There isn't room. You would have to clear the point at the end of the bay and you would still be on the water when you got there." Nevertheless," said Russ "seven". "Oh yeah, what was the wind doing?" Said Russ, slow and deep: "Seventy-five miles an hour."

Jack Malischewski snorted. "That's nothing." he said, "that was a breeze compared to a Queen Charlotte southeaster I got into one day in a Beaver. I made four passes before I got her pinned on the runway and managed to get up to the tiedowns in front of the terminus at Sandspit. CPA was coming across from Rupert and the pilot of the Canso flying boat also had to make four passes before he was on the runway. She still had too much flying speed and the wind picked her up and lifted her off the ground sideways, landing the ship on the grass strip beside the runway. She wind-skidded the whole length of the runway sideways and left a deep trough all the way up the side on the grass. She finally stopped eight feet short of the fence. There was no damage to the Canso and nobody was injured. Somebody made the suggestion they should have followed along after it and planted potatoes in the furrow."

Malischewski continued, "Roy was describing a mercy flight and that reminds me of one we had at Sandspit. We got a call from a fishpacker lying eight miles off the east side of Graham Island, south of Rose Spit. I went out as the pilot but when I found the boat, there was a heavy swell out there and I had trouble taxiing up to her stern. The skipper didn't help any because he kept manoeuvering to bring the boat to the aircraft and any fool knows the boat has to stay where it is and let the airplane do the work. Matter of fact, I had to climb out on the pontoon and yell at the skipper to sit tight. When I did get up to the stern, the skipper and an Indian fisherman-helper disappeared into the cabin and between them brought out a girl. Was she ever stacked! She was built! You could tell alright because all she had on was a pair of panties. She was unconscious. The two fishermen hauled her over the stern like a sack of fish, nearly dropping her into the chuck, and they propped her in the rear seat. She was out cold from drinking pinesol, a household cleaner-disinfectant. The skipper unconcernedly climbed over his fantail and took off. The Haida Indian was on board the Beaver on all fours, complaining about his heart. He wasn't worried about the girl and he had no more heart condition than I had, but with the fishboat gone I couldn't very well throw him overboard. So the three of us flew off to Charlotte City and the hospital, and when we got there the Indian just walked away and disappeared. All he wanted was a free ride. The girl died later."

Then there are the drunken passenger stories and every pilot has his favorite collection. Ninety-eight percent of them begin with "there was this drunken logger I remember" and ninety-five percent of the time they are right. Not that loggers are given to roistering any more than other coastal types but we pilots have it figured that loggers scare easily. This is a mystery since none of us would approach their dangerous jobs with a quarter mile pole. A man can get himself killed doing the crazy things they do in the bush. Anyway, when loggers have to fly into or away from camp, a lot of them prepare by getting stoned. How many have I hauled from base station washrooms and led aboard, big, but petrified?

Gordon Best still chuckles over his encounter with Audrey McKenzie, the company agent at Queen Charlotte City, while on one of his inspection trips. "Any problems?" he asked. "Not really," she said, "except one. How drunk should a passenger be before we refuse to take him?" Gordon explained there was a variety of circumstances and there was no hard rule. Someone with only a few drinks could be tricky. If women and children were on board more care had to be shown than if the other passengers were fellow loggers. Someone who was really stoned but benign could be carried with safety in the right circumstances. "Well," she said, in that haughty tone women can affect, "I think if your pilot has to carry the man down the ramp, then he's too drunk!"

Sometimes instead of sitting there wrapped in a boozy aura, a drunk becomes playful, like the one Jock Blakely had out of a logging camp north of Port Hardy. Since he was the only passenger Jock put him in the co-pilot's seat where he could watch him. Jock is a big,

153

easy-going fellow who can be tough when needs be. He was wearing his earphones, listening to the chatter of the base transmitter, watching ahead and concentrating on his flying, when the character grabbed the nearside earphone, pulled it out a foot and let it whap back on Jock's ear. "Hey," Jock exclaimed, "calm down. There'll be none of that!" A minute later he did it again and it hurt. Making no comment, Jock throttled back and landed right where he was—luckily for the passenger, at a little two-man camp. Jock shoved him out on the log boom, said, "I'll see you when you're sober," and took off. He picked him up next day and by then he was remorseful and apologetic. He has behaved himself ever since and has become a regular passenger.

Drunks are always changing their minds. I have seen plenty weave down the ramp, take one look at the airplane and stagger up the ramp again. The kind who change their mind once airborne are the ones to watch. All water-borne aircraft have coils of mooring ropes stored under the seats where they are readily available. On this particular day a Beaver was taking off from Campbell River and just as it was lifting off the water an inebriated gentleman decided it wasn't for him. He opened the door and stepped out but he got his foot tangled in a rope. It delayed him just long enough for the other passengers to grab hold and yard him back in. "God damn airline," he yelled. "It's getting careless. Leaving ropes lying around like that, somebody could get killed!"

Carrying on the way we do, out on the rim of the last frontier, sometimes it is hard to remember we are a link in the chain of global communications. And then I think of Wally Russell's story of the Scandinavian blonde doll.

Wally walked out of the Vancouver hangar one ·day to see his passengers aboard the Mallard sked flight to Ocean Falls. He looked them over as is our custom, wondering who to invite forward to the co-pilot's seat. Who was interesting today? A little old lady? A Crown Zellerbach company executive? A returning housewife after some town shopping? Who? Then he saw a petite blonde vision with a lovely figure. No doubt about it, she would be co-pilot this day. Cool it, he thought, lots of time to get acquainted. Once airborne he found that getting acquainted was a problem for she spoke little English. Now and then as they passed over the glaciers en route, she would look down and grin and then grab his arm excitedly and say something he finally understood to mean "just like my country." As he swung in over the dam at the Falls, losing altitude to land in the inlet, her excitement peaked. She was gesturing wildly down but all Wally could see out of the ordinary was a tramp ocean freighter warping up to the pulp mill dock. In those days the seaplane float was next to it and before Wally could make the usual opening gambit: "how about some coffee?" she ran up the ramp and along the dock to stand searching the freighter's deck. It was some time before he pieced it together. The girl had left Stockholm the day before and had flown to London. She had picked up a London-Vancouver overnight through flight and then had caught our Mallard to Ocean Falls. She had her timing worked out for weeks and she was on the button to surprise her officer-husband as he came down the ship's gangplank. Whenever Wally tells it now he seems more amazed at the part he played in an international reunion than the regret he might have had. But he always finishes the story wistfully, with:

"My, but she was attractive!"

I think of all the hundreds of stories I have heard about the B.C. coast, the one Bill Waddington tells is the best. Waddy, one of B.C. Air Lines' early ones, is now operations manager and senior pilot of Forest Industries Flying Tankers Ltd., headquartered at Sproat Lake, Vancouver Island. The company is jointly owned and operated by the five largest forest products companies in the province and its one job is to lay down water barrages over forest fires using rebuilt Martin Mars flying boats, veritable juggernauts of the air. The newspapers have tagged them "water bombers" and it is a phrase that Waddy dislikes intensely. He prefers "fire bombers."

The words are Waddy's:

"This is a 1949 story. I was carrying three passengers in a Sea Bee from Powell River to Vancouver and I noticed the oil pressure was dropping. Just before landing at Pender Harbour, I got a message off to Vancouver to send up another Sea Bee with an engineer. It arrived and the passengers were transferred and returned to Vancouver while the engineer, Hugh Thomas, and I went to work to find the trouble. It didn't take long to discover that gasoline had diluted the oil.

(The fuel and oil pump on a Sea Bee engine are combined into one unit and all that separates the gasoline from the oil is a small diaphragm. If it separates, the fuel gets into the oil thus reducing the oil pressure.)

"You remember," Waddy continued, "that the Sea Bee engine is behind so if anything is wrong the only way to tell is by the panel instruments. Well, just south of Sechelt, after we had changed the oil and got airborne again, the engine quit dead at 500 feet altitude.

There was no warning. It just stopped. I landed her all right but it was in rough water from a southeast 40. It was getting on to dusk because it was 4:30 of a February afternoon. Those damn waves were 10 or 15 feet high and it wasn't pleasant.

"Hugh put his head through the hatch to the outside and I heard him say, 'My God Bill, the engine's on fire!' We had one of those old Pyrene extinguishers and with both of us sliding around on top of the tossing fuselage, we managed to put out the fire. We found the fuel lines burned off so of course that was why she had quit. You know what the fumes were like from those old extinguishers. Hugh and I became nauseated and then we were sick as dogs.

"I got back to the cockpit and managed to raise Vancouver on the radio. I told them we had lost an engine and gave our location. Vancouver said it would look after us immediately.

"Then, somebody off the beach showed up in a boat. He had seen us come down with smoke trailing and he wanted to help. I thanked him but said we were O.K. and would just wait it out until another plane arrived from Vancouver. He waved goodbye and went off toward Roberts Creek.

"About 15 minutes later, we began to drift out from shore in the southeasterly and I called the tower again. 'It ain't rosy out here', I said, and was informed to keep my shirt on, that the RCMP boat from Gibson's Landing was on its way to tow us in.

"We were still damn sick and all the hatches and doors were open to ventilate the fumes. I guess because I was so sick, when I went to hang up the mike in the holder, I dropped it and it bounced into the sea. Now we couldn't communicate. I could receive but I couldn't transmit.

"The next thing that happened was a tug arriving alongside. He'd been hove to, sheltering behind Trail Island just out of Sechelt, and had caught our message. He asked if we needed help. We were still terribly sick but we said no, the RCMP was on its way from Gibson's. "Okay, fellas," he said, "good luck!" and then he left us.

"Time passed and we started to worry because the wing floats of a Sea Bee were never too watertight and we knew they would be taking water from the pounding we were experiencing. It was dark and we had drifted maybe three miles offshore. We were two scared fellas.

"An hour went by, then another hour, and after four and a half hours there was still no damn RCMP. We were into the really big seas now and I could see the wing floats were filling. I figured we had bought it. Then I spotted the lights of a Union Steamship and I got two flares from the survival kit and fired them off. The boat didn't see them, anyway, it didn't change course. I started flashing the navigation lights and apparently, as it turned out later, a boy on the ship saw them and ran up to the bridge to tell the captain.

"The ship came over and stopped on our windward side but as fast as she got stopped, the wind would drift us away again. This sort of nonsense went on for a long time until the captain thought to try and pick us up with his boom, plane and all, but he couldn't get close enough. The ship was riding pretty stable in big waves but we were on a constant elevator going up and down 15 to 20 feet. Finally, the captain decided to put out a lifeboat.

"Three seamen were aboard as the boat was lowered from the davits and when it hit the water they got what sounded like an old one-lunger engine going, but by this time we had drifted 200 yards away. Half way to us, damned if they didn't run out of gas! You can imagine two seamen rowing that heavy lifeboat in those big seas! It took them a half hour to get to us because meanwhile we were drifting away from them.

"We scrambled aboard when it caught us and I fondly patted the Sea Bee goodbye because I knew she hadn't much more time. The row back to the ship took another hour against the wind because we were still too sick to help, first from the Pyrene and then from seasickness.

"When we came up to the Union, they lowered the pulleys that come down from the davits. The idea is to hook them into rings at either end of the lifeboat simultaneously as the boat is rising on a wave. One guy got his end hooked and the other one didn't. Next thing we knew, the boat was hanging straight down with us holding on to the seats for dear life to keep from dropping into the water.

"When we got flat on the water again, the captain thought that idea no damn good so he ordered a rope ladder thrown over the side. Anything, I thought, just so long we get aboard your bloody ship! They called down to us to wait until the boat was on top of a swell, then jump. I jumped. Well, by God, I caught hold of the ladder all right but some stupid bastard above had forgotten to tie his end, so back I went into the lifeboat again on my ass, tangled up in coils of rope. It's a wonder I didn't break every bone in my body.

"They got another ladder and the captain himself tied it this time and one by one we finally got to the deck safely. The skipper took us to his cabin and then it turned out he didn't even have a drink. I think that was the crowning comedy. We went up on the bridge and the searchlight was trained on the Sea Bee. Just as we found her in the beam, she turned over and disappeared. We had been rescued none too soon.

"The RCMP? I found out later they had received the message and had headed out from Gibson's but had turned back when they ran into the high seas. They never advised anybody. Apparently, they just forgot about us."

It is three a.m. and my wife is tugging my elbow, but before we break up this bull session I have just one more. This one is about Bill Waddington too.

He had a good-looking girl-passenger in the co-pilot's seat of the Beaver as he went over the brow of a mountain where he was going to land in a little lake, 2,000 feet below. Bill turned to the girl: "Do you mind," he asked politely, "if I make a steep approach?"

"Hell, no," she said, "I've had all kinds. A steep one would be a novelty—whatever that is!"

Accidents
Happen

IT IS REGRETTED BUT ACCEPTED that our way of life includes accidents and possible death—so accepted we have become hardened to the daily toll of the highways and other kinds of tragedy that now beset a speeding world. Perhaps because there is still an aura of glamour to aviation, aircraft accidents are given bigger front page headlines and more graphic photographic coverage than justified, when it is remembered each new year brings an increase in the number of success-fully completed passenger-miles in excess of any other form of transportation. Automobiles, buses, trains and boats have an easy life in officialdom compared to the rigid rules of flight and the required maintenance checks under which the aircraft of the world operate.

At any given moment in the world today, it is estimated conservatively that over 4,000 airliners are in the air. When something happens to one of them, the headlines roll round the world. Any weekend in North America, enough people will die on the highways to fill six of the biggest jetliners and the story will rate six inches of type in one edition. The automobile is responsible for 200,000 deaths a year, world-wide. There were 746 murders in New York in 1967, better than two a day, which is enough for six jetliners, but you probably didn't know about them until you read it just now.

News media fatten on advertising billing to airlines but at the same time run dozens of air tragedy stories in a form sufficient to maintain the same tired blanket of suspicion held by the majority that "if man was supposed to fly he would have been born with wings." It is no wonder that better than 70 percent of North America's population has never been aboard an aircraft of any kind.

No one in the aviation industry is so naive as to expect news media to kill an air tragedy story or even underplay it. It is news and the news must be reported. The industry's legitimate complaint is that media over-emphasize and do not show judgment in using proper perspective.

In April, 1968, one of the coast's most well known pilots, Johnny Boak, with three passengers, was killed while gliding to the runway at Vancouver airport, caught in the turbulence wake of a 707 jet which had landed before him. The *Province* next morning, gave the story front page treatment and its last paragraph listed by date and type every fatal accident at the airport since 1947. If the newspaper's policy was consistent it would list every past automobile accident on the Fraser Canyon highway each time there is a fatality there but if it did the list would fill several columns and read like the casualty list of a small war.

There was a notorious example of muddled thinking by the Vancouver *Sun*, May 27, 1964. Page six that day carried a wide photograph, caption and short piece about a Pacific Western Airlines aircraft with some passengers aboard, that skidded while landing on the muddy, newly-installed strip at Hudson's Hope, nearby the Peace River Portage Mt. dam. It came to rest tail up, its nose in the mud. Besides the prop tips the only thing bent was PWA's pride. The photographer, in focusing on the buried nose, hadn't enough depth of focus to make the picture sharp all the way back and quite obviously a *Sun* artist had outlined the Pacific Western Airlines name along the fuselage to obtain sharper reproduction. On the opposite page that same day, there was a planted public relations type, human-interest story of a C.P.R. engineer who had just retired after 45 years on the railroad, and was about to embark on a round-the-world trip using scheduled airlines. The picture showed him boarding a Canadian Pacific Airlines jetliner, going up the steps, looking back at the camera, his flight bag hung on his shoulder. All identifying CPA lettering on the bag, on the steps and on the fuselage had been removed by an artist.

There is not one member of the industry from board chairman to airframe mechanic, from flight deck captain to the newest stewardess who does not wince when a tragedy story is over-emphasized out of all mature perspective. The implication is that somewhere along the way, somebody was not doing his best. Then, in the aftermath investigations, a second unfairness appears. It is on this unfairness I want to dwell but before I do you should have some background.

When the B.C. ferry *Queen of Prince Rupert* gashed her side on Haddington Reef off Alert Bay in fog, every officer, crew member and passenger was available for the investigation. It is comparatively easy to arrive at the cause of a train wreck in the canyon because all the evidence is still at hand. Most reasons for automobile accidents are readily apparent through study of the skid marks, statements of witnesses and/or survivors, and of the wreckage itself. Only rarely is any of this available to the investigators of aircraft crashes. When the wreck can be found, many times the pieces are briefcase size and only by piecing them together on a hangar floor can any theory of what happened be formed. Sometimes the key may be a piece only as big as a walnut.

Almost every airliner is now equipped with a tough little instrument called a flight recorder. It records on tape every manoeuvre of the aircraft from takeoff to touchdown, including the intercom talk between members of the crew. It is built and installed in such a manner that even if the ship is reduced to total destruction, it can be recovered and made to yield its taped secrets. The mystery surrounding air disasters is now not so deep it once was and in the majority of cases so far, the flight recorder's evidence has shown there was a malfunction of the aircraft itself and not of the crew.

While an aircraft is a shimmering thing of beauty it is also an amalgam of a million polished parts all subject at some time to periodic malfunction. Even the space ships, assembled in air filtered rooms by antiseptic men in lint-free clothing, are prone to the same hazard. A faulty one dollar bearing can neutralize a ten million dollar ship in a second. So many times we read of an airliner circling an airfield to burn off fuel so it could attempt a landing because its nose wheel wouldn't lower.

Then, there are the hazards over which the company or crew have no control, like lightning and turbulence, not forgetting the demented nut who smuggles a bomb on board. Of the last it is interesting to note an American police lab has developed an electronic sniffer able to detect instantaneously the smell of dynamite even through leather and surrounding packing. Perhaps some day it will be used at airports as a sentry alongside luggage conveyor belts.

Pilots who fly the coast are not faced with problems like high altitude jet streams, wind sheers, thunderstorms and lightning, and so far as I can remember, there has been only one bomb scare. By flying VFR, we avoid bad weather as much as possible. Our water-borne aircraft allow us to reach a safe landing on water in case of an engine failure. The pilots know the coast to a point that if forced down, and without reference to a chart, they can summon aid to their exact position. All these factors, allied with others, are some of the reasons why we enjoy an exceptionally high safety record. Despite them though, we do have a few tragedies.

After investigation, the company involved, as well as the Department of Transport, has with the odd exception, blamed them on "pilot error".

What is pilot error?

It is too broad a term encompassing a multitude of incidents that rapidly multiplying, bring about a situation from which a pilot can recover only with difficulty and possible luck. It usually leads to a crash and those who are prone to it are ones who fly only three or four hours a month.

Investigation usually shows the pilot was lost,

miles off his course; or he had attempted an IFR flight without instrument training; or had flown into strange country in poor weather; or had been advised of poor weather but had flown into it anyway.

DOT records show that besides poor visibility, the second principal reason for small aircraft crashes is the failure to apply carburetor heat. The control is like an automobile's choke and its one function is to apply more hot air to the carburetor intake. The intake, under certain conditions, is subject to severe icing that if allowed to continue prevents adequate air supply to the engine, resulting in engine failure.

Coast pilots are not novices. They are professional in most cases with thousands of hours of coastal experience. Sometimes they have to fly into frightful weather conditions but they do not fly into weather conditions beyond the capability either of themselves or of their aircraft. In winter when gales, freezing rain, snow squalls, low stratus and fog prevail, the weather is a deterrent but it does not necessarily prevent flying. Common sense, knowledge of the area and experience make the difference. In spite of these things however, the four worst air crashes in the company's history involving loss of life happened in bad weather and in each case the cause of the accident was ruled officially "pilot error."

I do not agree. It is just too easy to clean the slate with the eraser labelled "pilot error", specially when the pilot is no longer alive to defend himself. The term over-emphasizes the fact the pilot may have committed an error.

It must be remembered an element of danger is always present, as when piloting a fast boat or driving a fast car. The fact that speed is involved is reason enough. When you couple poor visibility with speed, the danger is aggravated. When the poor but flyable visibility suddenly becomes zero zero and unflyable, the pilot's judgment and reaction time has to be split-second to avert disaster.

Under such conditions, a normal flight would be at a low level, possibly following a familiar coastline that vanishes in an instant. If the pilot's flash decision is the right one, he continues to an alternate or if the water is calm he lands or he scrubs the flight and returns to base. If his instantaneous decision is wrong, the flight can end as a DOT statistic.

Does this constitute pilot error? I don't think so.

In reality, it is poor judgment under extreme pressure with split seconds working against the pilot. It is entirely possible in many cases, the decision the pilot made was right but he did not have enough split seconds left. Of course there is pilot error sometimes. I was involved with two accidents, both attributed to pilot error even though I was able to give my own evidence.

My point is the unfairness of the term. I suggest it be changed to *human error* specially when there is doubt about all the circumstances and the pilot is not living to file a DOT accident report with details. Every time a newspaper uses the phrase "pilot error" the general public undergoes more subtle brainwashing.

If "human error" was used instead, the emphasis would be where it belongs, as a normal happening of human life, rather than the connotation that a super-man was found wanting. Pilots are *not* supermen. They have mortgages and problems like anyone else. They do have super training but if there aren't enough split seconds left between the sudden appearance of a problem and eternity, all the super training is nothing. "Human error" is fairer by far.

My two accidents were minor, involving no injuries. The damages were less than $1,000. Over the years, I have periodically clobbered a dock with a pontoon or bent a wing tip against a fish boat or a wharf building. Everybody has, and they are not disasters. In the company's 22 years of corporate life, covering millions of flight miles and millions of passengers, there have been only six disasters.

One was a Norseman on floats making a routine landing, when the forward main strut from the fuselage to the pontoon gave way, overturning the ship in the water. Of the seven passengers plus the pilot, one passenger was trapped and drowned. The pilot couldn't swim but was able to free the rest before the plane sank. Investigation proved the cause and the pilot was absolved, in fact he was commended for heroism since the accident was in glacial water. If he had been given even one extra minute perhaps there might not have been even one casualty.

Our first major crackup took place on the Queen Charlottes early in the '50's. The pilot and two passengers were killed and three passengers survived. The DOT finding brought down the old judgment of pilot error. The pilot had about 1,000 hours flying time, knew the area well and was qualified on Beavers. He was ferrying his five passengers from Sandspit to a camp at Moresby, a short hop through a low pass. It was February, a bad month there, and after he got through the pass he saw a snow squall approaching from the southwest. When you are airborne, a snow squall is obvious and normally you try to fly around it. If the area is open and the squall is small, sometimes you fly through it. You are engulfed in snow for four or five seconds and that is the end of it. A large squall might have heavy turbulence in the centre and it might take up to ten minutes to get through—those you try to avoid. In this case it looked as if there was room on either side to go around but when he got close, he saw he couldn't circumvent. He was one minute's flight time from his destination and by the time he had reversed the Beaver's heading to get out of the squall, he had entered it and was caught up in 50 mile an hour winds. He lost altitude, was unable to regain and mushroomed into big stumps of the logged clearing north of the camp. He managed to switch off and thus prevented the loss of all lives on board. It was a case where there were not enough split seconds left.

A four-place Sea Bee featured in the next one. The pilot and three passengers headed out over English Bay toward Point Grey under special VFR conditions. Over the university on Point Grey, he took a bearing which should have put him on to the western tip of Bowen Island. From there he was to make his way up the coast. Part way across, he ran into moderate fog and descending to 25 feet above the water, continuing on his heading. It is unknown whether he miscalculated the heading or didn't allow for wind drift. He plunged into the solid rock shoreline of Bowen Island, killing himself and the passenger in the co-pilot's seat. The two in the rear seat did not have their safety belts fastened and were thrown through the roof to land on the rock. They survived.

The winter and spring of 1966 was a season of particularly rotten flying weather and there were several bad accidents. We had one on January 2 when one of the Grumman Goose flying boats, after attempting a flight out of Vancouver, was forced to return because of weather. Nearing the airport again, the pilot was instructed to hold over Point Grey for inbound traffic and after a little he was instructed to go in. As he did, just off the end of the runway he ran into a severe snow squall covering the tidal marshland and he went down into it killing himself and three passengers. Six other passengers survived after a long and harrowing rescue in the mudflats—a case which finally caused the Vancouver airport to secure a swamp buggy against the time when another such accident might happen in the same area.

In March, two months later, a Goose owned by Pacific Western Airlines crashed into Portland Canal, north of Prince Rupert, while encountering a heavy snow squall and attempting to make a landing to avoid it. The pilot survived but his six passengers were killed. He was flying into a steady 35 mile an hour wind but on encountering the squall, wind gusts between 50 and 70 miles an hour threw him partially out of control and unable to recover, he struck the water. The pilot still does not know how he escaped from the aircraft which sank suddenly.

A month later, in April, we sustained another fatal crash on the mainland, 200 miles northwest of Vancouver. The pilot and three passengers were killed. The aircraft was an amphibian Found, a five-place ship based at Port Hardy. The 25-year old pilot was well liked among the flight crews for his experience and ability. Periodic snow squalls were passing through that day, building up at the head of the inlets as constant snowfall. There were no witnesses, but piecing all the evidence, it was concluded a squall sharply reduced his visibility forcing him into a position from which he was unable to recover.

In 1967, we lost a pilot and a factory-fresh Cessna 185 on floats during a crossing of Hecate Strait from Kitimat to Sandspit. The pilot was as fully qualified as any in Canada with an instruments rating and years of experience. Ten minutes off Sandspit, he radioed, said he was ill and would need someone to fly him from Sandspit to Charlotte City, the nearest hospital. Those were his last words. Although a search went on for days, the wreckage was never found until much later, when a small part identified from such a Cessna model, was found on a lonely beach.

Of a conversation with a well known pilot of 25 years' experience, I remember one statement of his vividly: "We pilots are human and we are subject to human mistakes but we cannot make too many. Often when a problem comes up and it is counteracted at once, the problem vanishes. If it is not counteracted immediately, it becomes two problems and then almost instantaneously it becomes three problems. So it goes until the pilot has so many in the space of split seconds it is impossible to correct all of them and disaster follows."

I am not defending the actions taken by the pilots involved in the incidents outlined, but I do state honestly that I know every one of them would have exercised all their knowledge and years of experience attempting to ensure the safety of their passengers and aircraft, not to mention their own safety. Along with hundreds of other coastal pilots I know this to be true. We have all been close to a similar fate—but possibly we had that extra split second plus a divine guidance.

I have been involved in only two rescue attempts following air crashes. The one I will recount did not involve weather, malfunction of the aircraft, pilot inexperience, lack of knowledge of the area or anything else common to air disasters.

My log shows the time as 13:30, September 23, 1961 and the place, Campbell River, Vancouver Island. The dispatcher caught a barely readable, garbled message from Harry Brown, one of the Cessna 180 pilots, who was on a charter into one of the lakes east of Chilko, toward the southwest central part of the interior. Harry said he had spotted the wreckage of an aircraft in Dorothy Lake, just east of Chilko Lake, and there was a survivor. He requested that Air-Sea Rescue be advised in Vancouver and suggested we cooperate by sending a Beaver to bring out the survivor. I was airborne 45 minutes later at 14:15, carrying an extra jacket, a sleeping bag and a part bottle of rye.

I headed up Bute Inlet gaining altitude, more or less following the South Gate river at the head of the inlet, passing between Mt. Gilcrest and Mt. Grenville, both 10,200 feet high. At the head of the river, which begins on the south side of Mt. Good Hope, there is a slope requiring 8,000 feet altitude to clear. From there it was downhill into Franklyn Arm which is part of Chilko Lake. Just as I reached the lake, the Air-Sea Rescue Albatross flying boat arrived and I followed him up the valley 10 miles to Dorothy Lake. We circled and could see the wreck upside down in the water. It was clear the Albatross couldn't land because the lake is only a narrow slit among the 10,000 foot peaks, about a mile and a half long and a half mile wide, with bad approaches at both ends. After some yakking on the radio, we decided to return to Chilko Lake where I would pick up the Albatross' skin divers and then take them back to check for possible bodies.

I waited beside the Albatross while the Air Force

types put aboard an inflatable boat and three men and then took off, setting down on Dorothy Lake beside the turned-over aircraft, marked only by the bottom side of its pontoons showing above the surface. The skin divers, with their back-pack oxygen tanks, went down and vanished for ten minutes. When they surfaced they were holding a body, a big man in heavy hunting clothes and boots.

We took off for Chilko Lake at once and put the body aboard the Albatross, then I headed for Egg Lake, 40 miles northeast, where presumably Harry was waiting with the survivor. It was just dusk when I saw the Cessna on the lake and taxied up alongside. Harry told me he had hit a submerged rock while landing, holing one of his pontoons. He was astonished I did not have Ev, the survivor, with me. I had presumed he was with Harry.

Leaving Harry's charter fishing party of three tented on the shore, the two of us took off in the Beaver in approaching darkness to go back to Dorothy Lake where, so Harry said, Ev was in a hunter's cabin.

It was pitch dark when we arrived and the only glimmer was a faint ray reflecting on the water from a small light at the far end. I was really pleased with my landing on the glassy calm water. Taxiing to the light, we found Ev white and haggard, barely able to walk He said he'd seen me come down the first time and after picking up the body thought I would taxi to him to take him to the Albatross. He was at a complete loss when he saw me take off.

Harry got a fire going in the stove and we fried some cuts off a moose haunch, had a slug of my rye and tried to make Ev comfortable. He had a broken collar bone and was covered with bruises and abrasions.

Before he slept he told us his story.

Ev, and his friend Mel, were both captains of a major Canadian airline and Mel owned a Cessna 180. They were ardent hunters, knew the area, and had flown into Dorothy Lake every season for moose. They had arrived three days before, had shot a moose and butchered it and had stowed it aboard the 180, except for one haunch they would leave in the cabin. It is the custom in the remote parts of B.C. never to leave a cabin locked or unstocked in case someone in trouble should seek shelter there. On the day before being sighted by Harry Brown, they had taken off and were nicely airborne. Mel, who was pilot, began his turn at the end of the lake, climbing at the same time. The ship continued turning and nosed over. Before Ev could make a move, it hit the water from 200 feet with the engine on full climb power setting. The 180 flipped and Ev had to scramble to release his seat belt, open the door and climb up on the exposed belly. He thought Mel would follow but he was in shock and it took him some time to realize Mel was not out. He tried and retried to get back into the ship but was so numbed by the cold water he had to give up. He spent the rest of the afternoon floating gently down the lake on the overturned plane, hoping it would drift toward shore for he knew he was too weak to try swimming.

Late in the day he had drifted to within 300 yards of the shore and he decided to try to swim using the pontoon paddle as a buoy. When he reached the beach he made a half-mile trek through the bush to the cabin, got a fire started and began drying out. He knew he was in big trouble since their hunting trips lasted from three to seven days and they wouldn't be missed for at least a week. He had some food but his condition was poor.

Harry had spotted the 180 at noon next day and had landed and found Ev. He decided to beach his charter party at Egg Lake, return for Ev and take him to Campbell River. None of this had been understood in that first garbled radio message. The plan went up the spout when Harry holed his pontoon while landing his party on Egg Lake.

During the afternoon, I had been able to make contact with Campbell River and Vancouver, and DOT men were planning to arrive next morning from Vancouver. I planned to be airborne early to get Ev to hospital either there or Campbell River. By 9:30, we had Ev in a sleeping bag, sedated with four 222's I happened to find in my Beaver, chased down with four good slugs of rye and while it didn't cure him it sure as hell put him to sleep for awhile. Harry and I shared the other bag.

We thawed out next morning over the breakfast fire while frying some more moose and we were soon airborne for Campbell River, the weather anything but nice. There was light snow and I was worried about my fuel. Ev was propped in the co-pilot's seat and groggy as he was, he was watching my problems with a pilot's interest. That 8,000 foot hill ahead kept disappearing then reappearing in the cloud banks. I looked at Ev and he looked at me. "Well, what do you think?" I said. "Make a try for it, captain," Ev replied, we can't lose." So I did—I crawled up the sloping face of that semi-glacier like an ant on an ice cube, never quite knowing where the crest was. I was getting the old back hair feeling again when the cloud broke just at the top and we went sailing over to see a sheer precipice on the other side that was the South Gate river valley, on course Campbell River. The weather had become misty rain.

I heard the DOT aircraft calling me, asking for a weather report. I told him the weather was worsening and not to attempt. As I was speaking into the mike he appeared dead ahead coming toward me. He turned around and followed me into Campbell River and the three needles of the Beaver's three fuel tanks were all at zero when I taxied up to the base.

The epilogue of this story is the autopsy which showed that Mel died of a heart attack while making that climbing turn off Dorothy Lake. Here was an accident where there was no weather, no problem of any kind except human nature itself. Ev recovered speedily and was soon back at the controls of his big airliner. I saw him many times afterward.

Closing
the Hangar Doors

THROUGH THE COURSE OF TIME, rules and laws have evolved from problems occurring that needed solutions and to reduce the chances of the problems arising again. Man learns by his mistakes, the old saying goes. In every aspect of life, private or political, history shows how problems have brought rules and regulations still governing our lives today. One of the oldest book of rules governs ships and the men who work them. The Admiralty laws stem from hundreds of years of trial and error and with few exceptions they have been time-proven to be logical and sound.

Aviation is different. It has its panache but since it has been only thirty-odd years a major form of transportation, the rules are still being written. There were really none to follow in the beginning except those of navigation, and these adapted in principle, are the same as those that guided ancient mariners. This is one reason why specialized government crash teams swarm over a wreck, probing, re-assembling, reporting and recommending—all leading to improvement in aircraft construction, equipment refinement or handling procedure. Most aircraft accidents have only the mute evidence of twisted remains, flesh and metal, to speak for them and it takes almost inspired deduction sometimes to arrive at the cause of the disaster so another rule might be added or refined. Rules for aviation are being sharpened the hard way.

Aerial pioneers starting flights in farmers' fields, ended their flights in the same fields. In a little while, with the flights a little longer and maybe a little higher, they were terminating in somebody else's field. One of the first rules of flight stated: "The aviator shall not knowingly land in his neighbour's field." This led to the designation of areas for takeoffs and landings and finally to the present airports. By 1920, it was compulsory for pilots to be licensed and commercial aviation was on its way.

After World War I, a curious psychological reaction set in. The airplane had been heroic and glamorous during the fighting but with peace it became a one-time thing, with associations of violence and death. Surplus warplanes, not suited for civilian use, were dumped on the market under cost, leaving manufacturers with little demand for new aircraft. Flyers had to revert to a non-military status and those who tried to make aviation a civil career turned to barnstorming. When one was asked what was the most dangerous thing about flying, he replied: "The risk of starving to death." Those were the days of county fair exhibition wing-walking, stunting and sightseeing rides for fifty cents a minute.

It was also the day of visionary, indefatigable Billy Mitchell in the United States, who nettled President Coolidge into establishing a commission to study the best means of developing and utilizing aircraft in national defense. The Kelly Bill was passed in 1925 authorizing the calling of airmail service contracts. Byrd and Bennett winged over the North Pole in 1926. The Wright Whirlwind 220-horsepower engine was making longer, safer flights possible to the point that on May 20, 1927, a single one in a high-wing monoplane took Charles Lindbergh alone across the Atlantic for the first time.

The impact on aviation of that flight was explosive. From then on the world knew the airplane could span oceans, make the world smaller, shorten time, unite people with goods and services. It became apparent that more stringent rules and regulations were needed and gradually there came a complex web controlling aircraft construction, servicing, flight routes and behaviour during flight. These were followed by rules regarding government employed airport crews, tower operators and ground control personnel. Further regulations fattened the volumes with the inauguration of international flights and the involvement of passengers and crews with immigration and customs inspections. It has taken only some 35 years to develop the guide lines of today's aviation industry. Those regulations are proven by time to be logical and they help to contribute to the high safety standard, considering the millions of passenger-miles flown each year, each year increasing. It must be said it has not all been from the top down. The airline companies have also had a share of setting the rules, working in close cooperation with government departments.

Like most other industries, the aviation business is involved with many unions and their demands and restrictions fill more volumes to add to the complications. When to all of this are added the intricacies of the actual flights themselves, it must be admitted when an aircraft becomes airborne, its wings sustain a lot more than just the weight of the machine. The collective burden the operation supports is oppressive.

Jetliner passengers see none of this of course. To them, the pilot is a disembodied, cheerful voice in the overseat speaker and a happy flight is measured by the size of the martinis, the warmth of the stewardess' smiles and the cuteness of their fannies. The rigid discipline of the crew, the hours of ground crew preparation for the flight, the hours of flight crew readiness while it checked out the weather, the pattern, the alternates, the observance of every regulation imposed by both government and company—these things are not apparent and that is as it should be.

But, *our* coastal operation—that's a different octane altogether. If you want a drink you'll take instant coffee in a paper cup quaffed hastily at the agent's counter. If you want fannies you will have to settle for our bony, shiny-serged rumps as we go bent down up the aisle into the cockpit first having shoved a crate of machinery parts under your feet. We are steward, stewardess, flight engineer, navigator, radio officer, co-pilot and pilot all in one. The airliner captain's bulging briefcase becomes for us a handful of freight manifests. Our uniforms haven't seen the cleaners for a week because we've been too busy and the bit of gold braid on our cap emblems is mariner-green with sea salt. But by God, we'll get you there and back and we're just as conscious of the rules and regulations as any jet crew while we're doing it. We are more casual, that's all.

Away from our three main bases, where there is a manager and under him the agents, dispatchers, pilots and ground crews, the majority of our bases are controlled by the pilot-in-charge. Besides his small ground crew, he will be alone or he might have one or two other pilots. Here things get to the short hairs for not only is the pilot-in-charge responsible for the rules and regulations, he must also issue tickets, handle funds, keep the records, submit daily reports and think about public relations. It is like patting your stomach in two-four time, hitting your head to a rumba, tap-dancing to a time step and whistling "Dixie" all at once.

The bases are well apart from each other and radio is the only communication but the terrain between makes it an "iffy" proposition. As well, some of them operate on different frequencies. For years, I have been an advocate of a teletype communication system between the bases. The cost would be less than the telephone bill, and less time consuming than mail, but there is still no such system on the coast.

Like most others, our company is highly unionized but a lot of the pilots know all too little about affairs because of their remoteness. They hear about meetings too late, or the distance prevents attendance or in the case of a lone pilot, he is unable to leave his territory. This results in disunity and misunderstanding among the crews and it was a condition I resented. I am convinced that companies like ours, singularly far-flung, would be the better if all sections of both management and personnel formed an association under the Societies Act where each person would be a member. The executive would be drawn from each segment of the operations with representation from all the areas. This would allow utilization of the company printing machines, copying facilities and the powerful Vancouver transmitter, plus the use of the Vancouver base for monthly meetings. A lot of the isolation would vanish if this were done.

I am not anti-union but I do believe the seniority system is not the answer in our type of activity. With the continuing increase in business it is evident to me that unsuitable men are placed at certain bases not so much for the special ability required for a certain area but strictly on seniority or because it was their turn. I am not saying these men are not good pilots—of course they are. I am suggesting that a lack of knowledge of the area, coupled with a pilot's possible need for more management and sales training, can affect the progress of the company image.

So much has been accomplished in a comparative few years, providing service to thousands upon thousands of people in remote places, all done within the limitations, and sometimes *despite* the limitations, laid down by the Air Transport Board of Canada. It was renamed in '67 as the Air Transport Committee. It is a three-man body responsible to the federal Minister of Transport, formed in the mid-30's after a couple of airlines began operations. It has country-wide authority to grant or refuse operational licenses and routes.

The layman often confuses the ATC with the DOT, the Department of Transport. This body is responsible to the same minister but is a much larger organization because it governs the operating regulations of marine, rail and air, as well as pipelines. Even ski lifts must be licensed by it. It investigates all accidents within the different divisions. To both positions—

the federal Minister of Transport and the Chairman of the Air Transport Committee—I hope the day will come as do others in the communications business, when the two posts will be occupied by transportation men of long experience; that the ATC chairman will be a former successful airline executive who at least knows the difference between an undercart and a gocart. An essential would be he has to know the territory.

At first glance, the ATC provides a fair-shake-for-everybody treatment, Canada-wide, with equal judgments to all no matter the area. I am no authority on the situations in the rest of Canada but I do know my Pacific west coast and I state that what might apply to Ontario or the Maritimes, will not necessarily apply here. The coast's remoteness is unique and it takes one hell of a lot of money for even one company to set up a proper shop. The indiscriminate issuing of licenses during the late '50's, blanketed the coast with peanut-size air charter services to a point that none showed a profit. By 1963, there were 37 small companies flying about the coast, all struggling for the crumbs of the same pie.

Our company faced hungry years in the '50's, but instead of curtailing service it expanded and toward the end of that decade began a class 3 scheduled service using two, three and six passenger machines. Some schedules were twice daily, some daily and some every other day. They provided low fares in and out of isolated logging and mining communities. Prior to this all service was by charter which was and still is costly. The scheduled service allows a moderate fare for each passenger regardless of the number carried. If a fully loaded Beaver goes out, we make better than charter tariff. If there is only one passenger, while we use a smaller machine, we still lose money. It averages out by the end of the year and there can be a nominal profit.

One ATC ruling says a charter is to be paid by the individual in whose name the charter is requested. If five passengers want to go along, that is the charterer's privilege. He need pay only the flat charter rate. Any arrangement he makes with his "friends" does not concern the carrier. This is the loophole that detrimentally interferes with a licensed Class 3 company. It has become common practice on the coast but since it is not easy to prove, such small operators who so operate continue unchallenged. Anyone who does a lot of flying with the small operators would assist the industry by insisting on a ticket receipt for every flight. Many become pals with the pilots and feel they are helping the fellows get started, not asking for tickets. All that really happens is the money may go into the operator's pockets and the time may not be logged. Such situations then become a matter of ATC policing. When in '63, the company was able to have many of its Class 3 licenses upgraded to Class 2 protected licenses through ATC hearings, and on the grounds of past service, it meant the smaller outfits could not perform a charter along our protected routes we had spent years developing. But here again, through inadequate ATC policing, it has often been a futile exercise because the areas are vast and the number of small operators, many.

ATC policing on the coast consists of two overworked men who cannot begin to cover the area adequately, and always seem to be running hard to catch up while falling farther behind. The ATC inspectors live in Ottawa and make infrequent visits to the coast's bases and in the main they are necessarily cursory and routine. I have long wondered why they could not provide a short refresher course at the same time, to bring personnel up to date on new regulations and procedures. Periodic notices are mailed stating changes in procedures, and they are supposed to be entered into a master file but the theory does not become reality most of the time.

I think the ATC inspectors should be of the coast, know the coast and live on the coast. I think the position should be broadened to inspector-instructor and the work then include the many flying clubs. It is from these we draw many of the young men who will become pilots eventually.

And please, DOT, could we all wake up some Christmas morning and find all the lighthouses equipped with non-directional beacons? It astonishes many of us this has not yet been done. The beacons are relatively inexpensive, simple to operate with only minor personnel instruction and could be maintained with little extra cost to the government. These beacons would then allow our company and others to install modern automatic direction finders in all the aircraft, and while they still would not permit IFR flying, they would appreciably reduce the hazards of VFR flight in poor visibility, which is our damnable lot most of the time.

Most important on my list of DOT defaults is its failure to have so far not produced a foolproof SARAH (Search and Rescue Aircraft Homing) device, allowing downed planes to be found. It is 10 years overdue in the rest of Canada. On the coast and in the B.C. interior, it is 15 years overdue. The present SARAH is a good instrument but it is judged not to be foolproof by the Rescue Co-ordinating Centres, and it is not inexpensive. Why the National Research Council in Ottawa, which we are given to understand is a magnificent research institution and an asset to any country, has not been able to design a cheap, light, foolproof package is a mystery. SARAH is to an aircraft what lifebelts and lifeboats are to ships. One day more without such a piece of mandatory equipment is one day too many.

The present SARAH is not mandatory and is carried by only a few pilots as part of their emergency equipment. Sometimes it is not reliable in certain conditions and terrains, but it is the best there is until something better is available and every pilot should have one aboard just as he should have up to date charts. SARAH in its simplest terms is a small, battery-powered shortwave radio emitting a fairly powerful distress signal when activated after a plane is on the ground. It will pinpoint air search teams over the spot if they are tuned to the same frequency. Its signal cannot be changed and some types cannot be used for voice transmission. Its principal fault is it requires a survivor to operate it. If there are no survivors, SARAH is silent.

There is another very expensive device called the Crash Position Indicator. Its three components are fitted to become integral parts of the aircraft. It is released from the airplane electronically by the pilot pushing a button, or by a severe jar to any portion of the wings, cockpit or tail surfaces. When it hits the ground it automatically begins sending a distress signal on a frequency of 121.5 megacycles, VHF. It continues to transmit for 70 hours until the batteries are dead.

If an inventor is looking for another safety pin to invent—something useful this world really needs—a fortune in royalties is waiting if he can design such an automatic tell-tale which could become part of an aircraft's mandatory equipment for under $150. I often wonder why the Japanese, who have made such technical strides in developing mini-circuit, transistor radios, have not yet marketed such an instrument.

I would like to suggest another idea to the inventors. While a SARAH, even in a new form, would yield some information on the location of a downed aircraft, its signal is audio only. Based on experience in aerial searches, I think there should be some kind of visual signal as well. It is a proven fact that in the largest majority of air crashes, the tail portion of the aircraft remains intact. My blue-sky idea is a device built into the tail surface which would explode into action as soon as a certain degree of impact is experienced. Out of the tail would appear a blaze-orange, light plastic balloon that would be forced out by a pressurized hydrogen gas bottle, activated by the impact. As the balloon inflates it would climb into the sky above the downed plane, tethered to it by 7,000 feet of light fishline that would be contained within the tail on a small reel. Search teams would spot it easily like a barrage balloon over wartime London. Its name would be SARAB for Search and Rescue Aircraft Balloon.

Another item on the list of things I would fix, is the attitude of companies demanding the ultimate number of hours out of an engine before overhaul or change.

To show a profit in the flying business requires the maximum and efficient use of aircraft and personnel. Fact Two is the restriction that a pilot flying VFR can only fly 1200 hours a year. Fact Three is the adverse weather of the Pacific coast, making the attainment of the maximum hours almost impossible.

The 1200-hour rule, or 125 hours in any month, is a DOT restriction to protect the Canadian travelling public. It is a figure decided upon through the test of time, which when exceeded leads to a pilot's mental and physical fatigue, brought about by exposure to high frequency vibration and thinner air of undernormal oxygen content. CAPA, the Canadian Airline Pilots Association, puts the maximum for its members at 85 hours a month, with negotiable reservations for certain conditions. Major airlines have a 75-hour standard.

Engine operation submits to similar rules. For example, the Pratt & Whitney R985 engine that powers the Beavers and the Grumman Goose flying boats, are allowed by the DOT, 1,000 hours of operation between engine changes. During that time, the DOT requires numerous rigid inspections. Each 50 hours of operation, the engine gets a major tune-up like a car. Every 100 hours, the tune-up is more rigorous and parts like the carburetor, oil cooler, magneto and plugs are inspected and perhaps replaced. In this manner it is usual to reach 1,000 hours of operation without difficulty.

In our company, the pilot enters his daily flight time in triplicate in the daily flight aircraft log book and the original copy is sent to the main Vancouver base where the details are entered daily in the master aircraft log books. As well, the times are set down on a large blackboard under each aircraft's heading and this allows the maintenance superintendent to see immediately when an aircraft has to be replaced at an upcoast base with a minimum amount of downtime or non-revenue flying as the engine time runs out. The chief engineer is a licensed DOT inspector and it is his duty to see that the rigid maintenance program is followed and to submit the proof documents to the DOT at regular intervals.

It is known that some of the small operators do

not log all their flights, so when their log shows the engine to have operated 1,000 hours, in reality it could have in excess of that legal maximum. It is a hard matter to police. The public is entitled to the protection. This is another reason why everyone should insist on a ticket receipt for every flight in the interest of safer flying. I do not think the DOT has done an adequate public relations job in making the flying public aware of such facts.

Pilots are not expected to know much more about an aircraft these days than how to fly the thing, least of all the complexities about operating an airline in an efficient, moneymaking manner. When something is wrong with the radio I know there is something wrong with the radio, but I am not expected to know how to fix it any more. I can sense if something is wrong with an engine but I'm no aero-engineer or mechanic. Unlike a major airline captain who reports a possible malfunction and then walks away from the ship, not to see it again for weeks, but knows the trouble will be located and fixed, a B.C. coast pilot alone at a base with one aircraft, his engineer, his radioman and his agent, gets to know a great deal more about mechanics than he has to or is given credit for knowing. A close bond develops within his little team and he finds himself turning to, helping to correct the problem and learning in the process.

There was a little incident in Prince Rupert involving a Cessna 180 amphibian. The two junior pilots (by seniority only) complained they were not happy with its engine performance. They didn't know why, only that the sound wasn't right. The base engineer and I took it up and we could find nothing wrong. The next day one of the two pilots had an engine failure half way to his destination and had to force land with a blown cylinder. It was obvious the two who were flying the Cessna more regularly than I, were able to catch a change of tone in that engine and were correct in so reporting. My checkout flight with the engineer was not sufficient to prove them wrong.

I had a hairy few minutes over Juskatla harbour in the Queen Charlottes while flying a Goose. Just as I started my slow descent to a water landing I began vibrating severely to the accompaniment of a hair-raising clatter from the starboard engine. As I looked, I could see the thing trying to tear itself off the wing and then it burst into flames. Among other things, I got the starboard engine fire extinguisher activated, got the fire out and landed on one engine. I remember the agent saying afterward it was "kind of an oddball approach." I might add there were no passengers. There is more to the story.

A week before, returning to Rupert off the Charlotte schedule, I noted in the log the starboard engine didn't sound right. The engineer removed the cowling and found that No. 5 cylinder had blown two studs and was lifting from the engine casing. There are nine cylinders on an R985 engine, fitted to the casing in a circular pattern which is why it is called a radial engine. Each cylinder has its own head and is replaceable. No. 5 cylinder is the master cylinder of the nine to which the others are timed. The engine had logged 700 hours flight time, meaning it had 300 hours left before it needed to be changed. When 300 hours are converted to revenue time they represent a fair amount of money.

What would company policy dictate—change the cylinder and keep the machine airborne, or change the engine with the loss in the revenue hours? After several phone calls with Vancouver, and to the dismay of myself and my engineer, it was decided to change the cylinder. An engineer was sent up and after some complications, No. 5 was replaced. We static tested and all seemed well. That afternoon we test flew the crate for an hour and it appeared I couldn't be anything else but satisfied so I signed the log and put the ship back into service. It was the next morning that six of the nine cylinders blew over Juskatla resulting in fire and a near crash.

On one hand, I understand a company has to show a profit to stay in business. On the other hand, when something like a master cylinder blows, the sensible thing would be to lift the engine, send it to the factory for rebuilding, replace with a standby and keep the aircraft flying—and to hell with the hours of revenue time lost that are still on the log. In this case we lost a week replacing the thing, and following the Juskatla episode, another 11 days while a new engine was flown from Vancouver and replaced under adverse conditions at a logging camp. It all added up costing more than the revenue from 300 hours.

The company's pilot training program is one of the best available with the added dividend of so many types of machines to be checked out on plus the vast area to fly over and learn about. A new, young pilot with a commercial licence can begin on a small Cessna 172, move to a 180, go to a 185 and then to Beavers. From a Beaver he can graduate to the twin-engined Goose and then to a Mallard. It is only a question of time and seniority. He is checked constantly during the program, not only by the check pilots but by the base manager and the regular pilots. It is a tough training period and only about 50 percent complete it.

There is one aspect though I have long maintained needs improving. It is the transition from flying a straight seaplane on floats to an amphibious one on floats and wheels. There have been occasions, thankfully very few, when a pilot new to floats and wheels has made a water landing with his undercarriage still down. The result is quite a mess but not unfixable. The airplane is usually moving fairly slowly and it flips with a slow roll, so slow sometimes I've known a couple who were able to climb out of the cockpit and walk up on the downing side of the wing and never got their feet wet. Management of course, takes a dim view of such goings-on and unless an undercarriage malfunction can be proven, the result is another dismissal. There is absolutely no excuse for making a water landing with the wheels down, but it happens and it should not. The record shows in almost every such incident the pilot had very little time on amphibian aircraft.

When landing at a controlled airport one of the last remarks the tower controller makes in your headphones is: "You are cleared to land. Check your gear down and locked." An experienced amphibious pilot is constantly checking his undercarriage just as a careful motorist will check every so often that his emergency brake is off. It becomes second nature. The pilot might be a long way from his destination but unconsciously his hand keeps checking that lever to make certain the landing gear is up. On his approach to a remote landing, he completes his check and his final check is the undercarriage. He checks the pressure, the indicator, then visually, sometimes even saying to himself, as I do: "my undercart is up and locked."

I think the coast companies have lost some highly qualified men over the years—men who have landed with their gear down. The dismissals were correct but the thousands of invested dollars in their education could have been saved if they had received a more thorough checkout on one simple aspect—the amphibious undercarriage.

So it is that the rules for the flight are stringent with little margin for error. They are still being made. But with the rules there is also a need for a better understanding between unions and management, a closer working arrangement between management and its personnel, a better understanding and sympathy of the problems facing flight crews and ground crews in all phases of commercial aviation. It is coming but its arrival is too slow in comparison to the growth of the industry and the upgrading of equipment. No amount of regulations will ever rule out all the problems and hazards but the Class I airliner carriers are reaching that perfection quicker than the smaller operators. This is due in part to the designated routes they fly, under rigid control and surveillance the entire distances. As well, there are from three to five men in their cockpits representing a great fund of experience and knowledge.

We lag but we learn and to this we add a singular devotion to duty and to industry that builds morale in the team that is fierce and proud. Pilots such as Bill Waddington, Wally Russell, Peter Lauren, Al Eden, Roy Reaville have spent their lives in devoted service and are still flying today's hour as carefully as their first. Jock Blakley, Jack Malischewski, Gord Russell, Russ MacKinnon, Dave Stronach, Walt Winberg—I could go on and on. Then, there are the engineers who work in the damndest weather. I was never able to understand them. Possibly it is the satisfaction of knowing the machines they work on are aloft and flying well—men like Peter Groves, Norm Robins, Bill Kelly, Fred MacPhail, Denny Powley, Ed Richter, Jim Jones, Ned France, Al Ludl—all grease-begrimed for 15 and 20 years.

And for dedication you have to seek far to find a group like the heterogenous assembly of disembodied voices scattered the length of the coast who have served years at their shortwave transmitters giving weather conditions and forecasts, and being in general, the cheery voice in the dark when things are zero zero. They are women like Liz Schofield, Mrs. Kenmuir who is known all over the coast as Mrs. K., Mrs. Brennan, Tom Rait, Mr. & Mrs. John Fair.

So I close my hangar doors for the last time and I say goodbye to all of it and good flying to all of them. It saddens me to know I have ended a life among such staunch people. As a boy I had two ambitions, to be an architect and to play the accordian. I accomplished neither but I found a truly challenging profession that no one, least of all me, was ever able to master completely.

I met thousands of people, worked with hundreds who are unforgettable because they were a breed who stuck doggedly to the cause of self-satisfaction gained from a job well done, in a forbidding territory where the odds are against mere mortals who attempt exploits like aerial communication.

It was a pathless way of many paths for me—one million, three hundred thousand miles of the lovable and terrible, thrilling and hateful, beautiful and treacherous Pacific coast of British Columbia—but every mile was with dedication and service and most of all with *love*.

EPILOGUE

It is not the custom to add a publisher's footnote to a book but this time I think tradition breaking is warranted because the reader should know more about the author and the circumstances under which this book was written and because there is more to the story of aviation in British Columbia.

Here was a man.

Justin de Goutiere once met was never forgotten. Tall, handsome, courteous, understanding and knowledgeable, he was a person who was always welcome and one of the rare few who takes something away when they depart. Andy Marquis, featured in the Alaska earthquake story, says: "He was perfectly type cast for he embodied all the characteristics you ever imagined the storied Canadian bush pilot to possess. I often kidded him about his name because it just did not go with the rest of him. I told him he should have been French aristocracy with a name like that."

Gordon Best, his general manager, says now in reminiscence: "The name 'Justin' conjures in my mind the acme of the modern bush pilot. His unbounding enthusiasm for his work was unparalleled. He drove himself mercilessly and always had to be ordered to take a holiday. 'What will happen to *my* operation,' he would ask. He was always promoting new ideas for routes or services and was never loathe to inform management when he thought it was slow to react. He was an expert needler but if an idea was rejected he always backed the decision wholeheartedly. I wish there were more Justin's in the service."

Sydney Reynolds, his company's director of marketing, agrees: "Quit bitching, Justin used to say," says Reynolds. "Either do the job you were hired for, in the conditions you were hired into, or quit. Either way, let's get on with it."

Walter Russell, his operations manager, adds: "I can't remember how many times I had to replace a pilot working with him, because, as we said then, a clash of personality. Now I know it was only because of Justin's unceasing urge for perfection. For him, there was no progress in satisfaction."

Bill Waddington, featured in the story of the shipwrecked Sea Bee, as chief pilot for B.C. Air Lines Ltd., hired Justin in 1960 for just those attributes. "He was a good manager," says Waddington. "He was one of the very few you could trust completely and know the job was being done in the best and safest manner possible. He was a super salesman, selling the service both on and off the job."

"To our mixed emotions," adds Best. "One day, we came to the realization that hundreds of people along the B.C. coast were referring to the company as 'Justin's Airline'. Then we decided that since ours was a neighbourly service, maybe it wasn't such a bad idea."

And it wasn't a bad idea.

The first time I heard his name I was standing on the seaplane float at Ocean Falls, waiting for the plane to take me north to Prince Rupert. I was joined by a weathered fisherman, obviously an area old-timer. As we chatted, his crinkled eyes searched the sky down the inlet. He squinted at the sun, thought a moment and said: "Justin's late today." A few days later at Masset on the Queen Charlottes, 300 miles distant, I was on the ramp again waiting for an airplane. "Sure he will," said a lady in a housedress. "You can't bother the guy like that," said her husband. "He's done it plenty of times before," she argued, "Justin will pick it up for me, you'll see." When the Goose came up the ramp and that Gary Cooper type jumped from the door, she handed him a swatch of material and some money. "Sure," he grinned, "no problem." As I was disembarking from the flight in Prince Rupert, I asked: "Are you the Justin I keep hearing about?" "I guess that's me," he replied. "What did that lady in Masset want of you?" "To buy five yards of dress material like the sample." "Will you?" I inquired. "Damn right," he said, "I'm in the business of helping people and I do it any way I can."

Our paths crossed many times after that, for one reason because I made it my business to know him better. He intrigued me. He was different and he was honest. We became friends and when he was transferred to his company's Vancouver base we saw each other often.

Then, sometime during the summer of 1966, he began to drop things. A pencil would slip, a cigarette would miss the ashtray, a radio knob was stiff to turn, and as a responsible pilot should he sought a medical examination. Based on first findings, his company sent him to the Neurological Institute in Montreal. "I remember Justin well," says Dr. F. McNaughton, the director. "He impressed me as a man of courage and substance. How sorry I was to have to tell such a man there was nothing yet for him in medical science."

He had contracted a relatively uncommon affliction called motor neuron disease that progressively atrophies the motor nerve cells beginning with the furthest body extremities. It is thought to start from a long-implanted virus that wakens suddenly. Its mysteries have yet to be solved and it is terminal usually within two or three years. Only seldom does the disease arrest itself.

How do you sympathize with a man like him? He rejected pity, any indication of sorrow. "Hey, how about that!" he would say. "Nothing ordinary for me, boy.

They even wanted me to stay in Montreal as a guinea pig." But then, one evening around midnight, the doorbell rang and Justin was leaning against the frame. By now his hands had turned backward, spastic-fashion, his ankles wobbled and he had lost fifty pounds. "Can a drunken old man come in and talk?" he said. I think it was the first time in his life he was drunk. Now I know it was the low point of his life when he came to realize fully what lay ahead for him. It was time to lend more than lip service.

This book was born the following day. Justin had the gene of imaginative talent from his father who had been an actor, writer and artist and from his mother who wrote children's stories. "Why not," I suggested, "write about flying on the B.C. coast?" He began work two days later. His two oldest boys converted a bedroom into a cork-walled study where they pinned his wings, his charts and his pictures of better days. The telephone company installed a speaker phone, for he could no longer hold a telephone, and made him a "B customer" meaning he need only dial Operator and the dialing would be completed for him. He bought a dictionary, Barlett's *Quotations*, *Synonyms, Antonyms and Prepositions*, Roget's *Thesaurus* and Bernstein's *The Careful Writer*. He bought a tape recorder and he began to speak his memories.

Dictating a book, even in the best

conditions, is an almost impossible job. A normal writer sees his work taking shape on the typewriter. He paces and paragraphs and avoids repetition. He works from pencilled notes and perhaps an organization chart. He refers to many books and articles, flipping pages to find a fact or statistic he knows he has seen somewhere. Since Justin could do none of these things, his was the monumental task using memory only for by now he could no longer hold a pencil.

His enthusiasm was boundless. He had found purpose. At the end of the first week he phoned to say the first chapter was finished. Three days later he had completed the second, ten days later, the third, and a neighbouring housewife, Dee Bernard, offered to type the draft from his tapes. It was with a strange sense of anticipation and fright I began to receive the material—fright, because the content might not measure up and I would have to say so. The first chapter read was the story of the flight to Alaska and then I knew he had the stuff to do the job. There was much understandable repetition and it needed re-shuffling, paragraphing, refining and editing, but there was no doubt the therapeutic exercise had turned into an objective project I was certain would produce a useful book.

We entered a writer-editor relationship and in the following six months I came to know the meaning of courage as he weakened steadily. He was a wingless eagle in a wheelchair, helpless except for his mind which remained alert and knowing. After four rough drafts had been edited and re-edited, another neighbour, Kimbra Vryenhoek, typed the final clean copy — 227 pristine pages in a black binder and labelled proudly: "The Pathless Way by Justin de Goutiere". It was early August, 1968, when I hurried to him and laid the manuscript on his thin lap. He placed a twisted hand on it and looked at me. "My friend," he said, in a rasping whisper, "it's done. It's on the record — all those miles, on the record. The rest is up to you."

I never saw him again. He died with dignity ten days later. He never saw his book in print. He was 42.

~~~~~

Justin strove for perfection even as death approached. During the time we were awaiting the typing of the final manuscript he suggested there should be an epilogue chapter. "What's past is prologue," he said, "because by 1972 there will be a whole new look to the problem of frontier communication and the change has already begun. That makes nostalgic good old days of the book. I'd like to add one more chapter and bring the story up to date. It would be of better service that way." So he began again but we both knew he would never finish.

His voice was so weak by then, he could work only a few minutes at a time. This time he made some voice notes and from these, in essence, is what he wanted to say.

First, the problem:

Costs to operate float-equipped aircraft on the coast of British Columbia have increased to a degree such machines are now uneconomical. They have always been subject to saltwater corrosion and damage from wood in the water. Wind and tide have always created damage during their dockings. These are old problems but the doubling costs of maintenance are new and only a part of them can be passed on to the ticket buyer or freight forwarder. Waterborne aircraft have always had limited utilization because their speed is slow. At best they yield reduced revenue because they can carry only a few passengers. They have been and will remain trustworthy workhorses supplying communication on the coast but rising costs dictate there has to be a better way.

The problem is compounded because coastal industrial life is changing. *Production* and *sustained personnel* are the reasons. The day of the independent gypo logger with five to twenty-five men in a remote camp deep up an inlet, is coming to an end. There was a continual labor turnover but it was not a problem since the equipment was not complex. In general, a man only needed muscle to pull a saw, wield an axe or haul a choker cable. Now, portable steel spars, $100,000 cherry pickers, 100-ton diesel trucks and a lot more sophisticated equipment demand trained personnel. Today, men must be permanent, and expensive, high overhead machinery must stay hot. The portable spar for instance, needs a large logging area for it cannot be used on a steep slope where a six-man crew might hand-log. The pattern is changing to centralized logging by large companies and it is bringing about the instant towns of fine homes with the attendant amenities of good schools and excellent shopping centres where the new professional can have his family with him. The need for point-to-point communication is becoming less vital. It can be likened to the years when life on the coast concentrated around the major ports of call of the steamships.

Second, the solution:

Aircraft on wheels with their extra speed, extra utilization, greater passenger capacity and no complications from saltwater are the answer. Up to 1968, any commercial machine carrying ten to twenty passengers needed a minimum landing strip of 3500 to 4000 feet — an impossible thing to find on the coast. There are a few level places with clear approaches that could be developed but they are a long way from the densities of population. Now such service is possible with the advent of the de Havilland STOL (short takeoff and landing) turbo-powered

Twin Otter. Its minimum light takeoff is 350 feet! It can touchdown and stop in 275 feet! It can fly with floats but the necessary size of them so reduces the performance that the cost-versus-revenue factor becomes impractical. The STOL is crewed by pilot and co-pilot and carries 18 passengers plus baggage. Since it is worth in excess of $550,000, fully equipped for all-weather flying, it takes a lot of passengers to justify the expense and sophistication. Another new machine is the English Norman Islander with similar characteristics but only of 10-place capacity. Its equipped price is in excess of $100,000.

Now, if a large logging camp or instant town has 1600 feet of a straight, level road nearby, with clear approaches, it can be STOL-serviced. The short runway makes possible many new landing strips on the coast in places heretofore too short.

Float or seaplane operation will never disappear entirely but the bulk of that business will be maintained more and more by small independents who are not faced with the same overhead, labor costs and controls as are the larger companies. There are some 25 independent operators now.

Illustration is provided by B.C. Air Lines Ltd., largest of the coast operators. Since this book was written, it has sold its big base at Campbell River and given up its charters that once took its float planes into every remote inlet around that portion of

Vancouver Island and the neighbouring mainland. Realizing the changing picture, the company has sought permission to fly six different routes through the British Columbia interior to feed traffic into the mainline stopover points of Air Canada and CP Air. Its parent company, CAE Industries Limited, Montreal, has authorized $3 millions capitalization for wheeled equipment that will include the de Havilland Twin Otter and the Handley Page Jetstream — another new 300 mph machine carrying 18 passengers in DC8 comfort, needing only 3500 feet of runway at sea level.

..... All of this means that in British Columbia, airmen like Justin de Goutiere are either being retrained or phased out. First there were the real pioneers of frontier aviation like Ginger Coote, Russ Baker and Grant McConachie. I think Justin would like to be remembered as a Pioneer, 2nd Stage, for perhaps as present events forecast, that is what he was. I believe that is the real significance of this book.

Herbert L. McDonald
Publisher of the original edition

THE AUTHOR

JUSTIN VERNON DE GOUTIERE was a mixed-up Canadian. Born in Majorca, Spain, of a French father and Scottish mother, who were both born in India and brought up in England, he took his education in West Vancouver, British Columbia, graduating from its district high school in 1944.

He raised turkeys at 20, supervised a naval shore installation construction at 21, was a B.C. Provincial policeman at 22, drove a Greyhound bus at 23, became a Royal Canadian Mountie at 24, owned a restaurant at 25, sold it for a 700 percent profit at 29.

His passion for aircraft started with boyhood model-making. Active flying began in Quesnel, B.C., while a provincial policeman, when he and partner owned a Tiger Moth and an Aeronca Sedan for crop-dusting. At 29, he was a pilot for a coast construction firm, acquiring 4,000 hours flying time and an enviable knowledge of the coast. In 1960, age 34, he joined B.C. Air Lines Ltd. In the following 6½ years he flew 7,000 hours and 1.3 million miles, all but a few of them on the coast of British Columbia.

This was his only book and the talent came naturally. His mother's stories for children were published widely. His writer/photographer/artist father was well known in Vancouver through Theatre Under the Stars, CBC Radio and the School of Art. Both died within a fortnight when he was 22. His aunt is an American authoress of reputation.

Illness forced his early retirement from active life in 1966. He died two years later, survived by his wife, Anna, and their five sons. He was 42.